Walking To ...
Walking With ...
Walking Through ...

Sermons For Lent
And Easter
Cycle C Gospel Texts

Glenn E. Ludwig

CSS Publishing Company, Inc.
Lima, Ohio

BV4277
,L78
1994

Copyright © 1994 by
The CSS Publishing Company, Inc.
Lima, Ohio

Library of Congress Cataloging-in-Publication Data

Ludwig, Glenn E., 1946-
    Walking to— walking with— walking through : sermons for Lent, Holy Week, and Easter : cycle C, Gospel texts / by Glenn E. Ludwig.
        p.   cm.
    ISBN 0-7880-0005-5
    1. Lenten sermons. 2. Holy-Week sermons. 3. Easter—Sermons. 4. Sermons, American. 5. Bible. N.T. Gospels—Sermons. I. Title.
BV4277.L78   1994
252'.62—dc20   93-51081
                                                                    CIP

This book is available in the following formats, listed by ISBN:
0-7880-0005-5 Book
0-7880-0006-3 IBM (3 1/2 and 5 1/4) computer disk
0-7880-0007-1 IBM book and disk package
0-7880-0008-X Macintosh computer disk
0-7880-0009-8 Macintosh book and disk package

PRINTED IN U.S.A.

TO

Scott Garman,
who taught me to love public speaking;

Jim Shannon,
who taught me to love the church;

Jack Hoffman,
who taught me to love the ministry;

and,

the people of First Lutheran,
who allow me to share those loves with them.

Table Of Contents

C — Revised Common Lectionary; L — Lutheran Lectionary; RC — Roman Catholic Lectionary

Preface

One of the often used metaphors to describe Lent is "journey." We often say, "Our Lenten pilgrimage," or "journey." As we look at the gospel texts for Series C, that same metaphor seems appropriate. We are, indeed, on a journey during this season, and actually beyond the Lenten season into Easter.

Hence, the title for this sermon series. It seems to me, that as we journey into Lent, we are truly "Walking To" Jerusalem and the cross. We cannot read the story of Jesus without knowing that's where this journey of faith will lead. We are also "Walking With" a Jesus of Nazareth during this time. Especially in the events of Holy Week and the passion story do we understand the One whom we walk with. But the story doesn't end there. Easter is a time to celebrate "Walking Through." We join Jesus in his walk through the grave, from death to life.

So, we walk — to, with, and through. A journey that tells us more about who Jesus really is and who we are called to be as his disciples.

Before you turn to the 17 sermons in this series, allow me to offer a word of explanation about the preaching task from my perspective. There is a phrase going around liturgical circles these days that goes something like this: "Meaningful

worship needs to be Word Relevant and Sacrament Reverent.''
I like that phrase. It sums up for me part of what I understand to be the task of the preacher — relevant.

For preaching to be powerful and meaningful for the people we are called among, it certainly must be relevant, and that means that sermons must be place, time and people specific. The sermons in this series come from the context of First Lutheran Church of Ellicott City, Maryland. This is a fast-growing, suburban congregation. For me, sermon preparation is divided between textual study, reading others' sermons on that text, and being among the people for whom the message is intended. All of the theological study in the world is irrelevant if I do not know, understand, and love the people who have called me into their fellowship to share God's good news.

For many years I have used the resources of CSS Publishing. I have found the published sermons very useful in three specific ways: illustrations, a germ of an idea to expand upon, and even a direction I did not want to take the sermon I'm working on. I sincerely hope that the sermons in this series can serve the same functions for those who read them.

Finally, I would be remiss if I did not offer acknowledgments to those who helped, encouraged and supported this writing project. First of all, I need to acknowledge my indebtedness to all those preachers whose sermons I have read over the years. They have truly been influential in many ways: style, verbal skills, content, textual approach, and illustrations. Some of the ones I am about to name write for CSS Publishing and others do not. I gratefully recognize the influence they have had upon this sermon series: David H. C. Read, Edward Mangelsdorf, Durwood Buchheim, John Braaten, Carl Jech, Cherlyn Beck, William Berg, James Nestingen, William Hordern, Lowell Timm, Charles Mueller, and Herbert Chilstrom.

In addition, I need to thank the members of First Lutheran Church, who hear me preach regularly and have offered encouragement and wisdom to the preaching from our pulpit. They have opened their hearts to me and have allowed me into the sacred parts of their lives. Their stories are part of these sermons.

The staff of First Lutheran has been very supportive in the finishing of this project. I would especially like to thank Rosemary Fisher for all her help in the preparation of this manuscript for publication.

Finally, I need to thank my wife, Stella, for putting up with my fretting, stewing, and fussing about this book. She has been a constant source of encouragement and has helped me more than once to make what needs to be said relevant and meaningful.

May God grant you strength for your journey into these seasons. May the One who walks with us bring fresh insight and wisdom into your sermon preparations.

Glenn E. Ludwig

How
Jesus Began

Jesus taught his disciples, saying:

> *And when you pray, do not be like the hypocrites; for they love to stand and pray in the synagogues and at the street corners, so that they may be seen by others. Truly I tell you, they have received their reward. But whenever you pray, go into your room and shut the door and pray to your Father who is in secret; and your Father who sees in secret will reward you.* *(Matthew 6:5-6)*

Prayer — just the word elicits a wide variety of responses and feelings. Everything from the most pious of responses to the most piteous of excuses, the concept and practice of prayer has evoked much writing and discussion in Christian circles down through the ages. Most of us would profess fairly easily that we believe prayer is important. Most of us would have to confess, perhaps not so easily, that we do not pray as we should.

As we begin our Lenten pilgrimage this day, let us begin with prayer. And I mean that both literally and figuratively. Let us begin where Jesus always seemed to begin every venture and effort, with prayer. It is one of the Lenten disciplines espoused by the religious for years. But it is more than just

11

a discipline. So let us take some time, as we begin our Lent, to explore what prayer is, or is not.

Part of the problem, I suspect, about our failure to pray more frequently is our feeling uncomfortable in prayer. We don't seem to know "how to" pray. And because we get all hung up in the "how to" part, feeling inadequate for the task, embarrassed by the act, unable to address God as we feel we should, many of us simply don't. We don't pray.

Well, let's lay to rest the "how to" part right away. I found a wonderful poem that will help us put that issue into its right perspective. Listen to "Cyrus Brown's Prayer" by Sam Walter Foss:

> "The proper way for man to pray,"
> Said Deacon Lemuel Keyes,
> "And the only proper attitude,
> Is down upon his knees."
>
> "No, I should say the way to pray,"
> Said Reverend Dr. Wise,
> "Is standing straight with outstretched arms,
> And rapt and upturned eyes."
>
> "Oh, no, no, no!" said Elder Slow,
> "Such posture is too proud;
> A man should pray with eyes fast closed,
> And head contritely bowed."
>
> "It seems to me his hands should be
> Austerely clasped in front.
> With both thumbs pointing toward the ground,"
> Said Reverend Dr. Blunt.
>
> "Las' year I fell in Hodgkin's well
> Head first," said Cyrus Brown.
> "With both my heels a-stickin' up,
> My head a-pointin' down;
>
> "An' I made a prayer right then an' there —
> Best prayer I ever said,
> The Prayin'est prayer I ever prayed,
> A-standin' on my head.'"[1]

Part of the difficulty lies in the fact that we do not live in a praying world. It is a frightened and frightening world, but it is not a world that knows how to pray. It perhaps would like to pray, but many have given up on the task. It is a world that contains many who prayed once, but have given up the effort. There are many gifted people in this world, who do the best they can to meet the challenges of a troubled world and who seek to become worthwhile people and contributing members to society. But through it all there is a sense of isolation — from God — and because of that isolation, they feel alone in their struggle.

The real problem is that most of us were never taught about what prayer is and can be. We grew up confusing the God above and our discourse with God and Santa, from whom we asked many gifts and favors. Well-meaning church theologians haven't helped much either. Their definitions and discussions on the matter often leave us cold and confused. I even heard one well-known theologian in a seminar say: "Prayer is basically man in the totality of being stretched out to possess the transcendent, awesome God in the intimate inwardness of his deepest consciousness." That sure clarifies things and sets our hearts and minds to the task, doesn't it?

No, give me the wisdom of a Grandpa Rucker, one of the lively characters in Olive Ann Burns' book, *Cold Sassy Tree*. Here is wisdom born of experience. Says Grandpa:

> *"Another thang to think on: some folks ain't said pea-turkey to God in years. They don't ast Him for nothin', don't specially try to be good, and don't love nobody the way Jesus said to — 'cept their own self. But they go'n git jest bout as much or as little in the way a-earthly goods as the rest of us. They go'n have sorrows and joys, failure and good times. And when they come down sick they go'n git well or die, one, jest same as the prayin' folks. So don't thet tell you something bout prayin'? Ain't the best prayin' jest bein' with God and talkin' a while, like He's a good friend, stead a-like he runs a store and you've come in a-hopin' to get a bargain?"*[2]

Rucker got to the heart of the matter — our hearts. Prayer is being in communion with God, not something to be used when needs arise. Prayer is being in relationship so that God can speak to us, more than our pestering God with a grocery list of wants. Prayer is finding peace in the midst of troubles, calm in the midst of calamity, and love in the midst of our loneliness. It is not that we don't know how to pray; it is that we have lost what it means to be in relationship with a loving, hearing, forgiving and gracious God.

You see, in most of our discussions of prayer we often center on whether God answers prayer and how we can know that he does. But what if we learned that prayer, real prayer, has more to do with our ears, than with our mouths? What if we learned that prayer is not about my calling to get God's attention, but rather my listening to the call of God, which has always been there — constant, patient, and insistent? In relationship to God, if we are honest, God has always been the seeker, the initiator, the one to love unconditionally, while we flounder around with petty pieties and platitudes. In prayer, God is reaching out to us! Speaking to us! And it is up to us to learn to be polite enough to pay attention.

Can you see where this is heading? The big question is not whether God answers prayer or not. The big question is do we answer the call of God; do we respond; do we hear that invitation to join him on the road, an invitation that is always, always open.

Prayer — we need to see it not so much as a task we are called to but an opportunity we are given to be in communion, in fellowship, with a God who loves and cares for us. This Lenten journey we are on a road that takes us to a cross. And there is no fast way to get past that cross to Easter. We all must walk by Golgotha and the figure of the one who died there for us. Prayer can rightly put us in fellowship with the one who traveled that road for us then, and with us now.

Prayer is the only skill the disciples ever asked Jesus to teach them. They didn't ask him how to heal, to teach, to ask for money, to run meetings, to do miracles, to manage crowds, or to organize a movement. They asked him to teach them how to pray. And Jesus did — both in his "Our Father" prayer and by example. Prayer was the way he began every important step of his life — steps that lead to Jerusalem and a cross. Let us join him and listen to him. Amen.

---

1. Sam Walter Foss, "Cyrus Brown's Prayer," *Sourcebook of Poetry,* Al Bryant, editor, (Grand Rapids, Zondervan Publishing House, 1968), p. 524.

2. Olive Ann Burns, *Cold Sassy Tree,* (New York, Dell Publishing, 1984), p. 362.

The Easy
Way Out

One of the responsibilities that parents often have with children is the supervision of musical lessons. Getting the kids to practice is never easy. The first problem is just getting them to sit down to do it. Then, the second problem begins. Did you ever notice how easy it is to re-play the familiar? When you listen to those practices, ever notice how often you hear the same pieces over and over again? The prospect of struggling through a new piece seems like torture, so the temptation is not to bother — to be satisfied with the old, familiar songs, and not to struggle with the difficult, seemingly impossible new ones. The temptation is to take the easy way out.

But is this true only of children and musical lessons? I think not. All of us face days filled with the temptation to take the easy way out. Do we put on our sweats and walk or run this morning? No! It's raining, and we don't went to get sick. So, we snuggle down in the warm bed for another hour or two.

What about the issue we've been avoiding with our spouse? Now would be a good time to talk it out. But, no, the kids will be home soon and we will get interrupted. And anyway, maybe the issue will go away by itself. It sometimes does, you know.

And what about that pain in your back? You really should go to the doctor and get it checked. But . . . you're really busy right now, and anyway, it's probably just a pulled muscle.

17

We face situation after situation everyday in which the choice is not between good and evil, but rather between what is hard and what is easy. The temptation we all face, each day, is always to take the easy way out, and then to rationalize it away with a thousand and one excuses.

Is this a serious issue? At first glance, it would appear not. The examples used all seem fairly insignificant and the rationalizations sound reasonable. Who really cares, after all, if I choose to sleep in rather than exercise, or choose to ignore what's obviously a pulled muscle in my back? Is what I've labeled a temptation (to take the easy way out) really a big deal?

Well, theologian Helmut Thielicke thinks it is. In his sermon titled, "How Evil Came Into the World," he reminds us that "all temptations in life begin in sugared form."

Now we could spend our time together talking about "is there a devil?" But I don't want to waste our time. Call evil the devil, the tempter, Satan, the evil one, or the Prince of this world, as the scripture does. It makes no difference how we personify it, how we give it shape. There is evil in the world. It has been witnessed to since biblical times and we know it today in various forms and shapes. We've seen its ugly face in Auschwitz and in Bosnia, where genocide is the rule of the day and innocent people are killed for no reason other than they are of a certain race or creed.

Or look into the dark corners of our own hearts, if we dare. Do we know evil? Every time we hurt someone intentionally. Every time we try to make ourselves better than others. Every time we allow others to be hurt. We know evil.

And what of temptations in this world? Do we know them? You bet! Every day, in a thousand subtle ways.

Maybe we need to rethink sin. Maybe we need to think of sin in broader categories than just "bad things done" or "good things left undone." Maybe the most uncomplicated definition of sin we could give would be our inclination to take the easy way out.

Our gospel text for today offers a good way to assess our new definition. The devil offers Jesus temptations which

18

seem, on the surface, harmless enough. They are certainly not temptations to do evil. The devil is just encouraging Jesus to take the easy road in order to show the world that he really is the Son of God. Look, again, at these "harmless" temptations.

"Command this stone to become a loaf of bread." Temptation number one. Not a bad idea, really. Think about it. A lot of good could come from such a move. Changing stones to bread could move the world in a giant leap toward feeding the hungry masses. Thousands of lives could be saved. Isn't that worth some consideration? Think of the children we see with distended bellies. Think of the mothers who are too weak to feed their own children. Bread-making from stones could feed the world. Isn't God concerned with the hungry?

Or what about that second temptation? "Worship me," says the devil, "and to you I will give all authority over all earthly kingdoms."

Now, don't dismiss this one too quickly, either. There are some real possibilities here. Think about what it would mean if Jesus really were in charge around here. If Jesus had control, there would be no need for nuclear weapons of destruction. Wealth and resources would be shared more equitably. We wouldn't need a United Nations Peace Keeping Force to ensure the fair sharing of food supplies. It would be done, by Jesus, who had the power to make it happen. It's a plan that deserves some thought.

And what about that third temptation? "Jesus, throw yourself down from here" and let God perform a dramatic rescue. Again, think of the consequences. If Jesus did this, it would show that God can be manipulated to do what we want and what we need. It would show us once and for all that he really is here for us. And think of the consequences for Jesus' following.

Do you see the point of these three examples? The temptations were so subtle. And we could easily rationalize the outcomes! These "harmless" temptations could lead to Jesus being King of the World immediately and easily — no more preaching

19

to crowds on hillsides or by lakes, no more healing all those sick bodies, no more teaching to those who seem not to understand, and, most important of all, no cross to bear. It would have been the easy way out and it would have lead away from Calvary and death — but it also would have led away from Easter morning, and an empty tomb, and the death of death and sin, and the end of that real kingdom Jesus tried so desperately to explain to his followers.

The temptation of Jesus was to choose another way other than the cross. Maybe . . . maybe that is our temptation too.

The cross? We have to bear it, too. And every time we wish we could avoid it, every time we think there must be an easier way, we are tempted as Jesus was tempted.

Let's be honest, my friends in Christ. It is hard to be a child of God sometimes. It isn't always sweetness and light. There is evil in this world that must be confronted and that confrontation may be painful. The crosses that we may have to bear will hurt us, or drag us down, and we, too, are tempted to run from them, to take the easy way out. If we don't open our eyes to see the distended bellies and wide eyes of the starving children of this world, we don't have to share in their pain. Then, we don't have to feel guilty about that third television. If we close our ears to the cries of our neighbor who is so lonely and no one notices her anyway, then we don't have to care about her tears because we won't let her in and those tears will never soil our shoulders.

We fall to the temptation to take the easy way out in so many subtle ways — in our neglect, or ignorance; in our uninvolvement; in our blindness; in our prejudices; in our apathy — because the way of the cross is hard.

But, my friends, let us not forget: We do not carry it alone. The one who took up that cross in the first place not only has shown us how; in carrying his, he helps shoulder ours. He carried his and conquered it and because of that victory, he carries ours too. When our faith is weak, and trust is gone and we can't find God no matter how hard we look, he's there, carrying the cross, carrying us, through our temptations and in spite of our failures. He never takes the easy way out with us. Thank God!

In Death Valley there is a place known as Dante's View. There, you can look down to the lowest spot in the United States, a depression in the earth 200 feet below sea level called Bad Water. But from that same spot, you can also look up to the highest peak in the United States, Mount Whitney, rising to a height of 14,500 feet. One way leads to the lowest and the other way to the highest. From that point, called Dante's View, any movement must be in one or the other direction.

There are many times in life when we stand where the ways part and where choices must be made. It is often easier to trip along downhill than to walk the steady, or maybe rocky, uphill path. But the path uphill leads to a cross — an empty cross. And the one that walks beside us is the one who hung there and defeated it. Amen.

A Mother's Love
— A Godly Passion

"What is God like?" There probably isn't anyone here who hasn't struggled with that question. Theologians file it under "the nature of God" controversy. We all seek to know and understand this God that we worship and pray to and sing praises of. And we all know, at least in an academic sense, that our minds are incapable of comprehending God. Biblical images give us clues, however, about the nature of God. The image for today from our gospel text may unnerve some, and be a source of delight for others. But whatever, if we take it seriously, it will broaden, deepen, widen our understanding of who God is and how God works in our world.

One day, Luke tells us, the Pharisees came to see Jesus. "Get away from here," they warned, "for Herod wants to kill you." Now we are not told just what it was that bothered Herod. Perhaps it was that he thought Jesus might expose him, as had John the Baptist, and we all know what happened to his head as a result. Or, perhaps he sensed that Jesus would disrupt the status quo and rock the proverbial boat. And we all know that politicians hate rocking boats. In any case, his intent was not clear. All we do know is that he is after Jesus.

And Jesus' response? "Go and tell that fox for me," Jesus said, "I must be on my way, because it is impossible for a prophet to be killed outside of Jerusalem. Jerusalem,

23

Jerusalem, the city that kills the prophets and stones those who are sent to it! How often I desired to gather your children together as a hen gathers her brood under her wings, and you were not willing!''

And there you have it — another image for what God is like — like a hen gathering her brood under her wings. We need to ponder that image for a bit.

Have you ever spent any time watching geese and ducks? On vacation, I get to do that every morning. This past summer, there was a young mother mallard who had her brood. And it was interesting to watch how she took care of all seven of them. When anyone approached the lake, she became immediately aware and would gather her little brood together and hustle them along to hide in the reeds and brush that surrounded the edge of the lake. Once, someone went really close to get a better look, and she flew away. I was surprised by that at first — a mother abandoning her young. But then it became obvious what she was up to: She was offering herself as a decoy. She wanted the intruders to notice and follow her, away form her ducklings. She was willing to sacrifice herself in order to protect her offspring.

Now maybe we can understand the lament and the passion in Jesus' own voice. It is the cry of a mother who is worried to death about not only Jerusalem, but about all of us. Like a mother, Jesus sees far more clearly than do we, the children, the danger we are in. Like a mother, Jesus knows we tend to over-estimate our powers and are prone to go off on our own, leaving the protective wings, to seek our own excitement and adventure. And like a mother, Jesus chases after us.

Do you see the image? Like a mother, Jesus' love is so great that his all-consuming passion is to sweep us up into his protective arms. And although there are others in pursuit of him, namely Herod, Jesus, like a mother is persistent. He sticks to what his love compels him to do. He pursues his flock with a passion. His answer to Herod shows that: He has a little work to do in Galilee yet, a few chicks to sweep beneath his wings; and then, he is headed to Jerusalem, where he will, in essence, fly off from his chicks alone and draw God's judgment to him so that the jaws of death might sink their teeth into his flesh only, and not into his children whom he loves with a mother-hen's protective passion. Do you see the image?

Now, I know the image of God as a female can be disconcerting for some. Most of us have been raised with this patriarchal view of God. We regularly use the male pronoun in place of God. I know that I do. It is part of what I've heard and known since I was young. We think of God as all-powerful, all-mighty, all-knowing. Those images tend to re-inforce that maleness image. But here, in this passage of Luke, we have another image — a mother hen, with all her love and passion for her children, gathering them into her protective wings. And I ask you, isn't that image just as wonderful, and useful, and helpful in assisting us in understanding what God is like?

And this is not the only place in scripture where the female image is used to represent God. In fact, among the prophetic writings of the Old Testament, there are times when the feminine gender is used for the noun for God. And this image of a protecting bird is found in Psalms and Deuteronomy, as well as in Isaiah. And isn't it wonderful that God, who certainly goes beyond our human gender classifications, can be both male and female to us — can be both strong provider and motherly protector?

It is probably too much to expect for us to begin to refer to God with a feminine pronoun. But there is no reason, beyond our biases and upbringing, that that can't be done, for scripture itself does it and shows us how, when our images of God are expanded, our understanding of God can grow and deepen.

I must admit that I refer to God as she on occasion, especially when I don't understanding something "she" has done, because I normally don't understand women and their logic. And there are times when things happen that a rational man wouldn't do, so that must be God operating out of her female-side.

Seriously, I think it helps us to have this image of God as a loving mother. It helps us to understand God's longing for

223495

God's children, God's concern for their protection, God's willingness to sacrifice on their account. Maybe it takes this image of a mother to understand God's pain at our rejection of his/her love.

Think about it. It was not a spear forged by some pagan craftsman that cut into our Savior's heart. It was not the iron nails nor the crown of thorns that hurt him the most. It was the rejection by the very ones he had come to save.

You see, in this image of a loving mother, we have a mirror for our relationship with God. On the one hand, there is God's passionate efforts to protect and save us. And on the other, there is our persistent rebellion to that power, and opposition to that grace, as we seek to go our own ways in life.

And, although a mother's love can be rejected, it cannot be stopped. The love God has for us could not be aborted, either by a cross or by a flock of rebellious children. The cross of Christ becomes the symbol of arms outstretched that gathers all those in the world into a community of love and grace. Don't you know that a mother's love does not stop loving just because her love is not returned? Her love is not conditioned by response. Her love is! Period!

What a wonderful image for God — a hen gathering her brood — for what is the cross but the love of God that is so great, so passionate, that it is willing to die so that his children might live? What is the cross but the gathering under the outstretched arms of God of all of her children? What is the cross but God's compassion for his stray and straying children and his longing to gather them under his arms? What is the cross but a mother's love displayed as a Godly passion?

And that compassion has been an inspiration for godly lives ever since Calvary. One such story comes out of England in the 1940s. It seems there was a young woman who entered Oxford University with little focus for her life. She just did not know what she wanted to be or do. But she soon came under the influence of a colorful professor of English, a writer with a gift, named C. S. Lewis. She became a Christian through much of his influence.

She left Oxford, against the advice of friends and family, and began to study nursing. After five more years of rigorous training, she was certified as a nurse.

But her story doesn't end there, for her questing, Christian spirit would not let her rest with the way things were. You see, she ended up working on a cancer ward in a London hospital. Gradually, she came to realize that most of the doctors ignored the patients who were deemed terminally ill. With the result being that she watched many of them die virtually alone.

This troubled her greatly. She felt that Christian compassion needed expression to these patients in a visible way. She approached the hospital administration with an idea she had for surrounding those dying of cancer with friends and loved ones during their last days, rather than isolating them in sterile rooms with strangers. Her radical ideas were quickly rejected.

But undaunted, she decided to enroll in medical school to try to make a difference even though she was already 33 years old and would not graduate until she was 39. And she did make a difference, for she founded a movement that makes it possible for dying patients to live their days in a setting of love and support.

Cicely Saunders, out of Christian compassion and a sense of calling to help in a specific way, began a movement in England in the 1950s that later moved to America and that many of you know only too well. It is called the Hospice Movement, and it drew its inspiration from Jesus' own passion and compassion for his children — "as a hen gathers her brood under her wings."

My prayer is that God will continually come to us in new ways and in fresh images, so that more Cicely Saunderses among us can be moved and inspired to take risks to join in God's compassion for his/her children. Amen.

On Golf, Swimming, Gardening ... And Lent?

As the days lengthen (remember the meaning of Lent?) and get warmer, I begin to think about that game some of us play that keeps us humble — golf. It is a game I find frustrating, challenging and fun all at the same time.

This last fall, I was playing a round with someone who is quite good at the game. I am always open to tips and pointers and we were having a very good time, until we ended up behind a foursome that was playing in front of us. They had one golfer who was not very good. He would hit three bad shots for every good one, and we ended up watching him most of the day as we waited to play our shots.

It ended up being a good day for philosophy. "Do you know how to tell a really good golfer?" my friend asked. "The really good golfer is the one who can recover from a bad lie. Say he hits the ball into the bunker 20 feet from the green. He doesn't throw down his club like that guy up there and mentally give up. He just hunkers down, concentrates, and hits it out of there, right up to the pin."

And I got to thinking, there is a lot of decent philosophy in that observation: "He just hunkers down, concentrates, and hits it out of there, right up to the pin."

What would happen if we applied that to life? We all have those days when we make downright lousy shots in life. Every

29

business person makes some bad deals. Every parent makes bad decisions in child rearing. Every chef has a flop or two in the kitchen. Every preacher preaches some awful sermons.

The important thing, when you know you've hit a bad shot or you've made a bad beginning, is not to focus on what is past, not to fixate on the mistake, but to hunker down, concentrate, and hit the ball out in the right direction.

If we need a good biblical model for this philosophy, just look at Peter. Of all the disciples, the scriptures paint him as the most human — so human, in fact, that we almost wince for him a time or two. It seemed he was always saying something he would later regret or taking a stand he would have to back away from when more evidence came in. When it came to understanding what Jesus was going to go through — well, let's just say he flunked Theology of the Cross 101. "No, Lord," he said when Jesus said he must die on a cross, "this will never do." "No, Lord," he said when Jesus said they would all run away, "I'll never deny you." "No way," he said when the woman outside Caiaphas' house identified him as the follower of the Nazarene, "I never knew him." One bad shot after another!

But Peter didn't give up. He didn't give in to despair. Oh, he felt badly about what he had done. Scripture testifies that he went out and cried bitterly over it, but he didn't turn in his disciple's badge over it. He kept going on. He went back to the upper room with the others. When the women came in on Easter morning and said the Lord had risen, he raced to the tomb with John to see for himself. And he was there in the room when Jesus appeared to all of them, later that day.

When they went to Galilee, as Jesus instructed them to do, and Jesus called to them that morning from the shore as they were out in the boat fishing, it was Peter who stood up, put on his shirt, and plunged into the cold water to swim to shore and be there before the rest of them. Later that morning, it was Peter who walked along the shore with Jesus and was asked, "Peter, do you love me?" And Peter said, "Yes, Lord, you know that I love you" — all of this, in spite of the bad shots, in spite of the bad lies, in spite of all his troubles.

Maybe Peter's swimming lesson is also instructive for us as we walk our days of Lent together. In spite of what has happened to us in our pilgrimage on earth, in spite of the bad shots we have made, in spite of the times we have found ourselves in sand traps with our best efforts, the right instinct is to try again and to always keep our sights on God. For the past need not bind us: There is forgiveness and grace for that. And the future need not panic us: There is God's presence and Spirit for that. So what is called for is hunkering down, concentrating, and hitting our next shot with confidence, always keeping our eyes on God — for there is the strength, the courage, the confidence and the grace we need to go on.

The gospel text for today carries the same theme hidden in that parable of the fig tree. Notice what happens when the owner of the vineyard comes seeking fruit for the third time on that tree and finds none. The owner wants to cut it down and quit wasting time on it. It is a barren tree. But the gardener, the one who has the responsibility for the tree, begs for mercy. "Let it alone, sir. Let me try again with it. I'll plant some manure, and dig around it. I'll work with it. Give it another year." And the owner agrees.

Now, as you hear that story, who is the God-figure? Is it the owner, the gardener, or the tree, itself?

Well, it's a trick question in some respects, because, in telling this parable, Jesus seems to have cast two of the characters into the divine role. Who can deny that the owner of the vineyard, in the first place, is not a person to be reckoned with? This parable, by its very nature, is about judgment and accountability and crisis. But wait, here comes the gardener, the underling to the owner of the vineyard, to intercede. Now, who do you suppose he represents? Hearing the gardener's plea for mercy, the owner grants another year of life and it is the gardener now who will tend this tree to see that it produces fruit.

So, guess who we are in this story? And guess why we still live? Because of God's good grace and forgiveness in the intercession of the gardener on our behalf!

An important parable for us today? Well, I don't know about you, but in those days (and sometimes years) when I feel like that barren tree, I am glad that I know a gardener who will not only go to bat for me with the owner, but who will work with me in this next year I am given to see that I bear some fruit. And without making the obvious seem ridiculously simple, that is precisely what Jesus offers each of us today, this day, every day. He pleads mercy for us in our barren days and years, offers nourishment for us to grow in the grace period we are given, and stands by us with a love that will not let us be destroyed, no matter what life will bring our way.

The autobiography of G. Stanley Jones is titled *A Song of Ascent,* and is considered to be one of the spiritual classics. Jones was a great man: a missionary to India, a friend to Gandhi, a tireless world traveler, and a great writer and speaker.

Now, what is amazing to me is that this book was actually his third attempt at an autobiography. And he was 83 at the time. He had actually written two previous books but had been unwilling to publish them. The first, he said, was too filled with the little events of his life — things he judged not worth telling. In the second attempt, he tried to take the events of his life and to use them to philosophize about life in general. But even this, he decided, was not the right focus. The third time, he determined, he was going to begin with Jesus, and that's what he did. You see, what he discovered after two bad attempts was that he had been working backwards; he had been working from *events* to the *Christ Event*. And now, in his third attempt, he found he had it wrong. As he would say in his introduction to that third book: "Christ has been, and is, to me the Event. An African, after he was baptized, changed his name, calling himself 'After.' Everything happened 'after' he met Christ. It was so with me."

In his first two attempts, said Jones, he had been too *events*-centered and not enough *Event*-centered. In the third and successful book he concentrated on the Event and worked back to the events, understanding his own life in the light of Christ.

Now, as a writer, I know how hard writing can be. And to think that Jones threw away not one but two manuscripts, the second of which was 596 pages long, because he had made a bad beginning of it. Well, that is almost incomprehensible.

But Jones had learned, what all of us can learn from his example, that none of us has to stay with a bad beginning. None of us has to live with a bad shot. None of us has to be content with the mistakes of the past, and any guilt that may tie us to them. We have an advocate, a gardener if you will, who will free us from such burdens, who will give us courage to try again, and who will stand by us in the efforts we make to live as his people.

Maybe this day the owner will come. What will his judgment be? Fruit? Maybe it has been a barren year?

But wait . . . I hear some discussion about us going on. The gardener who has loved us from birth when he watered us into life and growth, the gardener is pleading for us.

And look! The owner has agreed.

Okay! Feed us, dear gardener, feed us. We are thirsty and hungry for what you have to give us. And we will seek to bear the fruit of your love and favor. Amen.

The Hands And
Arms . . . Of Grace

There is a wonderful story out of the Middle Ages that goes something like this. It seems people were putting pressure on the Pope, saying to him, "Your Holiness, this is the capital of Christendom. There ought to be only Christians in Rome. Let's get rid of the Jews." The Pope however, replied, "I don't know. Before I do anything, I will have a theological discussion with the chief rabbi of Rome. If the rabbi says the right things, the Jews will be allowed to stay. If he says the wrong things, they will have to go."

So they invited the rabbi in. The Pope dismissed all the Cardinals and said, "Rabbi, we are both theologians. Theologians deal in symbols. Since we use symbols in our communication, let this discussion be entirely in symbols." The rabbi said that was fine with him.

First, the Pope made a large circle with one hand and the rabbi responded by pointing to him. Then the Pope thrust out both arms to the chief rabbi. The rabbi responded by pointing to the Pope with two fingers. Finally, the Pope looked around for an apple and held it up. The rabbi went through the pockets of his long caftan and took out a piece of matzoh. The Pope concluded, "This is one of the finest statements I have heard of. Of course the Jews will be allowed to stay," and he sent the rabbi away.

The Pope, then, brought in the Cardinals and said, "I don't know what you people have been fussing about. I said to the rabbi, 'There is one church and it encompasses the world.' And he said, 'You are the head of it.' Then I said to him, 'There are two swords, the secular and the ecclesiastical,' and he said, 'You hold them both.' And then I said, 'There are foolish people who say the earth is round,' and he said, 'No, the earth is flat.' ''

The rabbi went home to his wife and told her. "You know, I haven't the foggiest idea what the fuss was all about. I got in there and the Pope said, "We've got you surrounded.' And I said, 'But we can get to you too.' Then he said, 'We can hack you to pieces,' and I said, 'We can poke your eyes out.' Then he took out his lunch and I took out mine."

Communicating with our hands and arms can be dangerous, it appears. But there are many times and in many ways that we do communicate with symbols and most of them are easily understood. For instance, what does this stand for . . . (peace)? How about this . . . (number one)? This . . . (okay)? And this . . . (power)? And what do we try to teach babies even before they can speak . . . (bye-bye)? How about this one . . . (bad person)? Or . . . (come here)? Or . . . (come here now!)?

I think there is a symbol present in the story of our gospel for today that is worth pondering for a few moments. The story is all too familiar. There was this son who got tired of working in his father's pizza shop, so he went to his dad and asked him for his part of the inheritance now, so he could go out on his own. The father agreed and the son was off. He immediately bought himself a Porsche 944, picked up Donna Rice, and headed for Las Vegas. There he bought drugs and booze and friends and when the money ran out, so did the drugs and booze and the friends. He ended up working as a busboy for Wayne Newton, so he could pay off his gambling debts, and he had to eat the leftover food on the plates he cleaned from the table to keep alive.

One day, while gnawing on a leftover rib, he realized how foolish he had been and wrote home to dad for help. Without a moment's hesitation and without reading the whole letter which was full of apologies and regrets, dad sent a first class plane ticket back home. The son arrived home and was greeted by dad with the biggest pizza party ever thrown in Baltimore.

Now, your translation may be different from that, but what symbol do you see at work here? Can't you just see the father running to greet that long lost son with arms outstretched and hands opened in welcome and love?

That's precisely how God loves us — arms outstretched, running toward us always, welcoming us home. Jesus says through this parable, "That's how God loves us."

You realize that we have misnamed that parable for many years. We know it as the parable of the prodigal son. Perhaps it would be best to rename it "The Parable of the Forgiving Father," for that is surely what it is all about.

And we have seen that symbol of the love and acceptance of God in an even more powerful way than in parable form. What about his ... (arms and hands outstretched on a cross)?

Think about those hands for a moment. They are pierced hands, bloody hands, pained hands. And they are spread in a gesture that takes in all the world. On that cross of Golgotha, to which we continue to journey these weeks of Lent, God was saying to you and me, "I love you *this* much!"

For, whose hands are they? God's Son, hanging pierced and bleeding from a cross, made the ultimate sacrifice for God's rebellious creation. "For God so loved the world (that's us, my friends in Christ) that he gave his only begotten son, that all who believe in him would never die but have eternal life."

We probably have trouble understanding such love. Our concept, our experiences of love, are never like that. We live in a world where we are rewarded for doing good and punished for doing bad. We grew up hearing that if you want something, you have to earn it, work for it, fight for it. That reward system of thought has always been with us. If we work

37

and get good grades, we will get into the best colleges and get our degrees and earn big bucks. If we brush our teeth and floss everyday, we will have good teeth and gums. If we please our employers, we can get a raise. And the list could go on and on.

But God takes that system and turns it upside-down and inside-out. On the cross, the hands and arms of grace spread out to encompass the whole world. God says, "You can't earn this. I'm giving it to you. Here is my son who is going to die so that sin and death won't have to threaten or worry or frighten you anymore. It is my ultimate sacrifice and you don't deserve it. But I love you *this* much!"

The world, you know, doesn't understand that grace. They don't understand the cross. For them, it is a symbol of failure, of pain, of defeat, of mockery. They thought they were doing away with a troublesome Jew and that would be the end of it. "Ha!" shouts God. "Ha!" And three days later, the world heard that shout through the echo of an empty tomb. The cross and the hands and arms of grace took on a new meaning. Now, instead of a symbol of torture and pain, we carry it as a symbol of victory, of God's power, of hope and salvation, of love — for you and for me.

The prodigal sons and daughters of God know only too well how beautiful is the sight of the one with open arms and hands welcoming us home. I have known many prodigals, have been one a time or two, but none stands out more than the freshman coed at the college where I served as chaplain for five years. I helped recruit her for the school. Her older sister was one of my students and actively involved in the chapel program.

When younger sister hit campus, she decided to break all ties with her sister, with me, with the chapel, with God. She played prodigal and she played it as well as anyone I've seen. She drank, did drugs, slept with any upperclassman in pants, skipped classes, had rowdy parties in her dorm room — the whole thing. I gave her her space. But every once in a while, I'd drop her a note to let her know that I was still around and that I cared and that God cared through me. She was in serious academic trouble in three months and her lifestyle was as low as it could get.

One day a rap came on my office door, and I opened it to find my friend with tears streaming down her face. I'll never forget her words to me as she rushed into my arms: "I've come home."

In the embrace that followed, the arms of grace, the arms of God, encircled us both and she knew she was home — where love and grace and forgiveness are waiting.

I don't know about you, but I thank God for those arms and hands of grace, for they have welcomed me many times when I have been lost and hurting.

Look at that cross, my friends. Those arms welcome you, too. Amen.

On The Cross-Road

Some people never grasp a new thing; they simply don't know what to do when confronted with a new idea, concept or invention they have never been exposed to before. This may have been one of Jesus' main problems with the people of his day.

A number of years ago, as the story goes, oil was discovered on some Oklahoma property that belonged to an old Native American. All of his life, the man had been poor, but the discovery of oil made him a very wealthy man. And one of the first things he did was buy himself a big Cadillac touring car — you know, the one with the two spare tires on the back. However, because he wanted the longest car in the territory, he added four more spare tires. He bought an Abraham Lincoln stove-pipe hat, added tails and a bow tie, and completed his outfit with a big black cigar.

Everyday he would drive into the hot, dusty little Oklahoma cow town nearby. He wanted to see everyone, and be seen by everyone. He was a friendly soul, so when riding through town he could turn left and right, and even turn all the way around to speak to folks. And it was amazing, but true, that he never once ran into anybody, or over anybody, or onto anyone's property. Why? Because directly in front of that big, beautiful car, there were two horses — pulling it. Some people never grasp a new thing.

41

Some people do not know what to do with new things, or new ideas, or new inventions until someone comes along with enough patience to explain it to them.

I had a friend who worked construction one summer while going to seminary. The work was hard; the pay was good; and it was great being out in the air everyday after sitting in dusty, stuffy classrooms for the better part of his life. But it was a foreign world to him. It certainly wasn't part of his seminary curriculum, although any pastor that has ever been involved in a building project believes that it probably should be.

The project my friend was involved in was the building of a six-story apartment complex for senior citizens. He was hired as a mason-tender. Now, how do you learn to be a mason-tender? Well, it's kind of like learning to be an usher or a lector or a communion assistant. It's called these days, O.J.T. — meaning, on-the-job training. You learn as you go. And you can just imagine that the bricklayers, the masons, were only too glad to give a greenhorn with soft hands help.

So it was that my friend was sent from one corner of the construction site to the other in search of a "left-handed door stud for a door that opened inward." He spent the better part of the day looking for one, with the help of amused masons. Finally, the foreman, with a gleam in his eye and a smile tugging at the corners of his mouth, took my friend aside and, with patience and a good deal of self-restraint, explained some things to him — like there really ain't no such animal as a "left-handed door stud for a door that opened inward" despite the drawing of one my friend had to help him find one.

It's sometimes hard for all of us to grasp new things, especially because new things are not part of our past experience. My friend could find his way around a seminary library; but on a construction site, it was a new world, and he was lost for a while, until someone explained things to him, showed him what to do and how to do it, and helped him understand what was expected of him.

Jesus went around doing something of the same thing for people as that foreman did for my friend. We are limited in our understanding of who God is and how God relates to us. And some people, in Jesus' time, had some pretty crazy ideas. They had trouble grasping who God is, so, Jesus went around doing a lot of teaching, preaching, and showing. He did a lot of healing and said, "Look here, this is what God is all about: helping the poor, the blind, the lame, the leper." Jesus went around playing with children, and said, "Look here, this is what God is all about: Unless you have the faith and love and trust of these little people, you can't grasp really well who I am." He went around talking to winos, prostitutes, cheats, tax collectors, and said, "Look here, God loves you and cares about you. You are an important person because you, too, are one of my children." And Jesus went around telling stories about sons who take up their inheritance and go out and blow it on wine, women and song; ending up slopping the pigs and going home to a father who waited and celebrated his return. He told stories about lost sheep and a shepherd who risks life and limb to find them.

Because people had trouble grasping who God is and how God deals with people, they had to be shown and told in many ways over and over again. Because God is so great and our understandings so limited by our experiences and past, our ideas about God are always in need of expansion, for we will never be able to fully comprehend the greatness of God.

But that's why we are here, isn't it? To hear again the story of how God loves us; to try to grasp some more of God's greatness; to struggle to understand how God deals with you and me, with our lives, and how then, we are to relate to those around us.

And so, Jesus told stories, parables, played with children, prayed with mourners, talked to adulterers, healed the sick to show, to demonstrate, to explain, to live out a way of life he called the kingdom of God. And by so doing, we grasp something about who God is for us.

Take, for example, the gospel lesson for today, the parable of the tenants in the vineyard. In the account of the story, three servants were sent by the absentee owner of a particular vineyard to collect the rent from the tenants he left in charge. It is a simple story, somewhat gruesome in its detail, but it tells us something about God. These three servants were beaten and thrown out. So, the landowner decided to send his son and the son gets killed.

Let's stop right there — what's the point? The story doesn't make much sense, does it? Why would anyone in his right mind, after having sent three servants in a row all of whom get beaten up, why would any loving father send his son after seeing what happened before? The landowner must be nuts! We can't grasp the point very well because it is sheer foolishness.

And yet . . . and yet . . . even though it doesn't make sense, the son goes and gets predictably killed.

Even though it doesn't make much sense, the God of creation who sent prophets to Israel and watched them be stoned for trying to show and tell people a better way; even though it doesn't make much sense, this same God sent his son — and he got predictably killed. And we still sit and shake our heads and don't get it. Why would God do such a foolish thing? Because God loves us, his people, his creation, so much, that God will take the risk. That's what Jesus is saying in this parable and it doesn't make sense, and it's hard to grasp, but God loves us — to the point of risking his son; God loves us to the point of a cross.

Even though it doesn't make much sense, God takes a risk on you and me. In the middle of our impatience with our children, God still loves us. In the middle of our making fun of classmates, or ridiculing a friend behind her back, or gossiping about a neighbor, God still loves us. In the center of our sin, even as we kill his son over and over again through our own acts of hatred, pride, jealousy and arrogance, God still loves us. Tell me, does that make any sense to you?

And so, Jesus told us a story — a very foolish, illogical story — about God's love and God's risk and God's action in sending his son, Jesus the Christ. Why would God take such a foolish risk? I can't comprehend it all; my rational, small mind can't totally understand how and why God operates the way God does. But it has something to do with God's profound love for creation and, specifically, for you and me. How else can you explain that God accepts us even while we are sinners? How else can you explain that God forgives me over and over and over again for the same thing that I know darn well I shouldn't do, but just can't help myself?

God surely must love us because he puts us in this vineyard of his, and gives us the freedom to work at it, and even gives us the freedom to harm his messengers and each other by acts of hatred and violence. And yet, God sent his son in *love* — for you and me. What a perfectly illogical, irrational, profound thing to do!

So, what is our response? Take that parable apart any way you want to, and we are the tenants in the vineyard. And what are we to do? — to tend the place, to bear fruit, to care for each other, and to thank the owner with the fruits of our labor.

Even though we aren't as faithful as we should be; even though we, too, kill God's messengers with our lack of love and respect for one another; even though we often want no part of the work of this vineyard — God still loves us.

God still takes the risk with us today. He still sends his son. He still calls us to be accountable for the work of his vineyard. And he continues to come to us to give us his love, so that we might learn how to risk loving one another.

Someday ... someday ... perhaps the impact and the profoundness of God's grace and love and forgiveness will move us in the depths of our being to live the new life he offers for us.

Someday.

Maybe, this day. Amen.

45

A Parade
That Gets Ugly

The city was in the mood for a celebration.
 Streets jammed with people from all corners of the world.
 The Holy City was a frenzy of activity;
 voices pitched a little higher than normal;
 children scampering about with greater abandon;
 people talking and greeting and gathering.
The crowd had formed,
 larger than a normal Passover crowd;
 large enough to worry the Roman soldiers;
 large enough to worry good old Pilate.
Listen to the crowd:
 "Can you see him?"
 "Look, here he comes!"
 "Hail, Son of David!"
 "Finally, someone to free us from these Roman butchers."
 "Blessed is he who comes in the name of the Lord."
People are putting palm branches in his path,
some are even putting their own robes down.
 "Oh, what a great day this is for Israel!"
 "The Romans will be crushed;
 we will be free once more."
 "Hosanna, Jesus is the King."

But it is not to be,
    at least, not according to the crowd's expectations.
      "Listen, he is going to speak again.
        Maybe this time he'll outline his plan of attack."

          "The kingdom that is coming is the kingdom
            of God."

        "Oh, no, not that kingdom of God business again.
        Tell us where we sign up for your great army,
        "I'm ready to fight!"

          "The kingdom you can enter is the kingdom of
            God."

        "Bring in the revolution, for crying out loud!"
        "Can't you see that's what we want?"

          "The kingdom you can share in is the kingdom
            of God."

    "He's a phony; he's not a general!"
    "All our dreams, our hopes, our prayers — ruined!"
    "Get rid of this charlatan — we don't need talk about
      kingdoms, we need action!"
    "Send him away. Lock him up!"
    "Yeah, give us Barabbas, at least he's honest —
      he steals our money;
      this one steals our dreams!"
And the choice is made,
    crosses erected
      the punishment executed with typical Roman precision —
        pound — nail into flesh
        pound — nail into flesh.
And there he hangs — "The King of the Jews" —
    to be mocked, to be scorned, to die.

That scene is replayed over and over and over again —
    rejection, disappointment, crucifixion.
Listen! It's happening again!
    Another rejection of God — this time the hammer is called
    "apathy."

"God? Jesus? So what? Who cares?"
"What difference does it all make?"
"Life is a _____ and then you die."
"Religion is just a crutch for the weak."
"Crucify him!" Pound — nail into flesh.

But there is more. What about our rationalization, our excuses?
"This Jesus is too religious, and I'm no fanatic."
"Pray, Lord, have me excused, for I have bought
a new ox (car?) and I must examine it."
"Listen, preacher, I work six days a week,
and Sunday is my day of rest."
Excuses. All kinds of excuses,
often magnificent excuses, noble excuses,
mazes of excuses, high sounding phrases, poetry even.
"But God, I can't spend the time right now.
You see, I have this dinner to prepare and some more
Easter shopping to do and the oil needs to be changed
in the car and ..."
"Crucify him!" Pound — nail into flesh.

The reality of the cross.
Think about that for a moment.
Is it a vision of some bygone era?
A symbol of torture used by cruel people in an alien
culture?
Or ... or is it a reality which we know only too well;
even today,
even now.
The crosses of despair,
and emptiness,
and meaninglessness,
and loneliness?
Do we know such crosses?
We've hung on them, haven't we?

You see,
we, who have waited to see the parade of Palm Sunday,

we know the passion,
not only of the week ahead,
but the passion which put Christ there in the first
place.
And for those who reject his cross,
Ours become so much heavier.
for without him, we carry them ourselves.

Can't we see that in his death,
ugly as it is,
life is made possible?
Because now, forgiveness has been made real,
love has become flesh,
grace has been poured into the very fabric of our being,
life is offered.
As we walk in that parade this holy day,
do we really realize where we will end up?
And do we really know what that means for our lives?
Amen.

A
Towel

He took a towel . . .
> That night before the Passover was to begin,
>> stripped off his clothing, filled a basin with water —
>>> and washed his disciples' feet before their last supper.
> An act done out of time, an act repeated at the wrong time,
>> stirring up memories of an enslaved people,
>> the land of Egypt,
>>> and the Passover that set them free from Pharaoh's bonds;
>>> only to face a watery wall, which God opened for them —
>> A door to the wilderness and a 40-year struggle that seemed worse than slavery.
> The Promised Land with its milk and honey was a fanciful dream in those days.

He took a towel . . .
> insignia of the servant,
> symbol of the slave doomed to a life of menial service,
>> a kind of living death.
> The slave knew his future, her fate —
>> to be turned out when her usefulness was ended,
>> to wander and beg for food, remembering how good his master had been to him,

until he lay down in weakness and dried up in the desert,
returning unnoticed to the earth,
dust to dust.

A towel . . .
so out of character for the Son of Man, the King of kings —
to do for others what had been done for him a few short days
ago in a house at Bethany,
when a jar of precious ointment was opened,
evoking memories of the birth of a child,
and the visit of wise men bearing gifts of gold,
frankincense, and myrrh.
No manger here, though; no mother's loving arms.
This was the beginning of a wake.
One who sought refuge from sin and guilt shed copious tears,
washed his feet in a torrent of remorse,
and wiped them with her rich, luxurious hair,
wrapping them in a shroud,
as if to hide them from the world, or to shield them
from nails, and the sting of death.

A towel . . .
such a humble act; a step toward the cross.
The disciples should not have been surprised.
They were with him as he entered Jerusalem on that
lowly beast.
The Prince of Peace went through the Golden Gate of the
City of Peace in character — meek and lowly and sitting
upon a colt, the foal of an ass.
Despite the acclaim of the crowds,
the palm branches, the flowers, and the clothing spread
in his path, and even the Hosannas,
that's when the letdown, the end, began.
Perhaps some began to think that a stronger man would have
to take over the leadership of the little band,
make it into an effective instrument of power and pressure;
The Passover message had to be reframed and sent to Rome:
"Set my people free!"

Only a real man, a genuine king, could lead this movement;
a servant armed only with a towel, and words,
eliminated himself.
He was politically dead already!

A towel . . .
It had to be done before supper,
before his suffering began at that table;
when he had to tell them what he knew of one's betrayal,
a sellout for the price of a slave.
He was acting out his fate; Judah had already doomed him
to the ultimate slavery — death.

His fate was sealed —
he would not be whisked off to Egypt
as Joseph had been when his brothers stripped him of the
coat of many colors and sold him into slavery.
He lived to forgive his people and feed them in a foreign
land when famine threatened them with extinction.
Joseph gave them a new life, refuge for the exiles,
and the hope of return to the land they loved.
But this Servant could expect no sojourn in alien territory —
only a cross — to show the world what happens to
revolutionary slaves.
A cross — warning to all to accept without question
the power of princes and rulers.
A servant-slave makes no protest; he simply accepts his
fate in silence.
The towel told the world that Christ had learned the lesson
which the Romans were teaching the world —
Caesar is king! Long live the king!
Death to all who would make the earth a place of peace
and freedom for all.
Jesus had come just for this, to serve God
and to suffer for it —
to set all people free from sin and death,
to show what incarnation really means when God
becomes human, and lives and dwells among his people.

A towel . . .
such a lesson —
for a towel tells us what we can expect on this night
when we remember and relive the last supper
and celebrate the New Passover, the Passover of gladness.
The Present One, the living Lord, the Host of this table,
is the Servant —
who did this for us, for the forgiveness of our sins.
He offers us the only food he had to give them —
himself —
Bread — his body broken,
Wine — his blood shed for all,
the true staff and stuff of life,
and the key to a life of loving service to God and all
people.
And when we have eaten our fill this night — at this table —
he clearly says to us:
"Do as I have done to you.
Take a towel and follow me!"

Amen

Good Friday
John 18:1 — 19:42 (C)
John 19:16b-22, (23-30) (L, RC)

Reflections On
"O Sacred Head"

Note: This sermon is more effective if the following three things are done. First, print the words to the hymn "O Sacred Head" in the bulletin for the day so that people can follow along and meditate upon them. Second, have a choir or a solo voice, or a combination of the two, sing the phrases as they come in the sermon. And third, use plenty of pauses and times for meditation throughout the sermon. A deliberate delivery is needed.

As we gather on this Good Friday, it is appropriate for us to focus on the cross, and particularly, on the One who hung there. To help us do that, we will use that most solemn hymn, "O Sacred Head, Now Wounded." I invite you to meditate on each phrase as outlined in the bulletin. Let the words and their meanings penetrate to the deeper parts of our lives and allow them to speak meaningfully to us. Listen, feel, experience the hymn anew this day as it points us to that cross and the One who hung there for us.

O sacred Head, now wounded,

His head was, indeed, sacred. We know that. We confess Sunday after Sunday that he was God's son.
But "sacred" means set apart — that which is intended for a holy purpose. So, it wasn't just that he was God's son;

he was God's son who came with a purpose to his people. And surprisingly enough, amazingly enough, it was a cross, an instrument of torture, that made that head sacred. Here was the fulfillment of God's great plan of salvation. Here, at the cross — a head, bleeding, wounded, sacred, because now, in God's mysterious way, he would fulfill that for which he had been created.

But, it is hard to understand that, isn't it? With the sky turning black, and the hopes of a people dashed like fragile glass upon rock, it is hard to comprehend the sacredness of the wounds. Until . . . until we know, not just with our heads, but with our hearts and souls as well, that those are his sacrifice, his love-gift for us.

With grief and shame weighed down,

Do you remember how he stood outside Jerusalem and with great emotion cried out, "Jerusalem, Jerusalem, how often would I have gathered you to me as a hen does her chicks, but you would not?" We understand something of that kind of grief. It is the grief of a parent for a lost child, or for a prodigal that has yet to come to herself, or for love given to those we have helped to bring into the world that goes unreturned. Grief so intense, that the very heart is torn in two.

But what of this shame? It did not belong to him, but to all those who put him on the cross; to all those who could not look him in the eye as he hung there; to all those who refused to believe that he really was who he said he was; to all those who could not grasp the meaning of this new kingdom he preached; to all those who thought it was over. The shame is ours and even *that* he took with him to bury in the grave.

Now scornfully surrounded
With thorns thine only crown:

They thought to make fun of him, dressing him in a purple robe, placing a crown of thorns on his head. There was no angel chorus singing, "King of kings and Lord of lords"; no one to proclaim him the Prince of Peace. And yet, the centurion looked on his lifeless form and said, "Surely this was the Son of God." They looked for an earthly king who would solve all their problems. Instead, he told them, "I have come to live your problems, to give you the strength to cope, and I will solve the only problem that really counts, where you stand with your Father in heaven."

Now, I ask you, what kind of a king is that?

> *O sacred head, what glory,*
> *What bliss till now was thine!*
> *Yet, though despised and gory,*
> *I joy to call thee mine.*

It is easy to follow this Jesus during the good days. The healings, the teachings on the hillsides, the wonderful stories he would tell. We loved them. We loved him. He said we were to go out and tell the good news that God's kingdom had come. It was great. We believed him. We believed in him.

Now, look at where it has led. The joy of anticipation has led to the sorrow of defeat, or so it seems.

But it is hard for us to stay sorrowful, because we know the story doesn't end here. We know what's ahead — a real victory, a real joy. But don't you see? This is part of our problem. We want to jump there and avoid this scene before us. We don't really understand why this has to be. We don't want to think about crosses and sacrifice and atonement for sin because ... because maybe we will have to carry one sometime; maybe God will call us to sacrifice; maybe to follow Jesus means this.

> *How pale thou art with anguish,*
> *With sore abuse and scorn!*

Have you ever looked into the face of someone in great pain? The face, indeed, becomes pale. But any pain we have ever experienced is nothing compared to the cross, a pain that was not just from the nails, the thorns, the beatings, the suffocation, but also from the rejection of those he came to save, the desertion of those who were closest to him, the derision of those who claimed to be closest to God. "Pale" is not strong enough a word. He looked like death. He became death for us.

> *How does that visage languish*
> *Which once was bright as morn!*

It was his eyes. In all the representations of Jesus I have ever seen, from paintings to movies, it was his eyes that always fascinated me. Whether they really were like we picture them, we will never know. But we do know that people we know who are alive, and spirited, and exciting have those kinds of eyes.

I picture Jesus with a twinkle in his when he taught his disciples, a twinkle of love and joy; I picture those eyes laughing when surrounded by children. I see them on fire when confronting the Pharisees and Sadducees.

Did the light, the joy, the fire go out while he hung on that cross? Could any life show through such agony? Some have said that the last word he spoke, "It is finished," was not the last gasp of a dying man, but the triumphant shout of one who had overcome. Surely the eyes twinkled with a secret we could not know for three days.

> *The grief and bitter Passion*
> *Were all for sinners' gain;*
> *Mine, mine was the transgression,*
> *But thine the deadly pain.*

They don't say much about crucifixion in the scriptures. Those people knew what it meant to die on a cross; we can only imagine. No one who studies crucifixion can ever really be the same. Isaac Watts would write: "See, from his head, his hands, his feet; Sorrow and love flow mingled down." Those are poetic and descriptive of Christ's work for us, but in plain English, Jesus bled. Real blood.

Just a day earlier he told his disciples: "This is my body which is broken for you; this is my blood which was shed for you." Did they know at the time what he was talking about? Do we really know? "He was wounded for our transgressions, bruised for our iniquity" means that he took on punishment that rightfully belonged to me, to you. I don't ever remember once being punished for something I didn't do without making a fuss about it. Jesus only said, "Father, forgive them."

What language shall I borrow
To thank thee, dearest friend,
For this thy dying sorrow,
Thy pity without end?

There is only one language that can begin to express true and proper thanks, the language of the obedient life. I saw a cartoon that showed a woman singing, "Take my silver and my gold, Not a mite will I withhold," and at the same time she was thinking "Of course, I mean that metaphorically, Lord."

So many of our great hymns express this thought of being absolutely and completely Christ's. He even said, "If you love me, you will keep my commandments." How many times have we asked God to reveal his will to us and at the same time were thinking of a million reasons why we shouldn't, couldn't do what God revealed to us?

Oh, make me thine forever,
And should I fainting be,
Lord, let me never, never
Outlive my love for thee.

I used to think that walking with Jesus was an easy journey. After all, I have known no other kind of walk all my life. But the older I get and the more complicated life becomes, I know that walk is not like any normal walk through life. It involves a cross; it means living with the burden of my sisters and brothers on this planet; it means living a different kind of life than the world would lead me into.

But for those who take this journey with Jesus, it is a journey of discovery. We discover that happiness cannot be made or bought. We discover that peace is a gift. We discover that peace is a gift. We discover that life holds wonder and love and joy ... because the journey doesn't end at the cross.

We don't like to stop here very long. But we must, for only by that cross, can we know forgiveness and restoration and renewal and grace.

Lord, let us never, never outlive our love for thee. Amen.

Living In The Nonsense Of The Resurrection

Did you hear that? Did you hear what was just read — the account of Jesus' resurrection? Did you hear the reaction of those closest to Jesus? Luke 24:11 — Listen again: "But these words seemed to them (the apostles) an idle tale, and they did not believe them."

Isn't that a fascinating verse to include in the account of the resurrection? Here we are, come to celebrate the greatest event in the history of the world. Here we are, come together to rehear the greatest story ever told — that death has been defeated, that sin holds no power to destroy us, that a kingdom awaits us, that there can be new life now. Here we are, and what do we hear? We hear that those closest to Jesus during the three years of his ministry, those who heard him preach on hillside and beside water, those who had shared in miracles, those who had broken bread with him as only friends can in the intimacy of the upper room, those who had heard him teach with patience about the kingdom of God, now we hear that when they heard the amazing story of the empty tomb, they thought it was nonsense!

Does that boggle the timbers of your faith a bit? It does mine. I have always had this image of the disciples — the true followers of Jesus. These were the eye-witnesses to Jesus' ministry. If they hadn't shared what they saw and heard, we wouldn't have, today, the story of Jesus to tell. And here they are, these people of faith, these whom Jesus told about his new kingdom he was establishing, these whom Jesus tried to tell about what would happen after three days — they thought it was an ''idle tale.'' It was nonsense to them.

But you know what? They were right! The story the women told them is nonsense. Who ever heard of someone regaining life after being declared dead for three days? Why, that's preposterous. The brain cells would have died, the body would already be decomposing. It is nonsense to think that someone who went through the agony of crucifixion and had the life, breath and blood squeezed out of him could suddenly have enough strength to walk out of a damp, dark tomb. And what about that huge stone rolled away from the tomb's entrance? Explain that! This whole resurrection story is so much nonsense — it defies medical explanation; it goes against rational thinking; it just isn't possible!

But it happened! Dear friends in Christ, it happened. It is nonsense, but it happened.

I believe one of the biggest problems with Christianity is that people want to take the nonsense out of it. I've heard radio preachers and television evangelists and all manner of Christians try to tell me that Christianity makes sense. That it's the easiest, most natural thing in the world to believe in Christ. I've been told and preached to and almost convinced that being a follower of Jesus is simple, that the stories of miracles and healings and the accounts of Jesus' life, some of them amazing to me, are easy to accept. I've been told that it's logical to believe in someone who walked this earth almost 2,000 years ago in an obscure corner of creation, someone who performed miracles, who fed 5,000 people with a few loaves and fish, who raised a friend from death, who forgave a scorned woman at a well her sins. Tell me, is it logical to believe in something that happened so long ago, so far away, something that defies medical, scientific, rational explanation?

I'm sorry, folks, I don't buy it. I'm afraid I'm in the camp with the disciples. It is nonsense. For me to believe any of this would be for me to accept what isn't possible. Believing in an event, in a story, that is so radical would have to change my perception of life. If I believe the women's story who ran from the tomb that first Easter morn, then I'm stuck with believing something so new, so different, so radical, that my life will have to change, to be new, different, radical as a result of the belief!

I don't care what anybody says. It isn't logical, rational; it doesn't make sense to believe in Jesus, the Christ. It is nonsense, this story of resurrection. And it is precisely *because* it is nonsense, precisely *because* it defies explanation, precisely *because* it is radical, that my life is dramatically changed by it. Because Jesus the Christ lives, I too can live — that's radical. Because of Jesus the Christ, I can love my enemy; I can pray for those who persecute me; I can turn the other cheek when someone slaps me; I can give when others hurt — that, my friends, is radical. It is not the way of the world. To be a Christian is not to be a rational, logical part of this world. To be a Christian means to live in the nonsense of the resurrection, to live a radical new life because the tomb was empty. Jesus lives and is here now with us. Because of what he did, love can triumph over hate, goodness over evil, truth over lies, hope over despair.

We *are* new creatures — radical, nonsensical people who live believing an amazing story. We are new creatures in our baptism into this Christ of the empty tomb. We are new creatures — with love to share, with a story of hope to tell, with forgiveness to embrace our neighbor, with hands and hearts that can reach out beyond our own selfish concerns to that person who needs us. We are new creatures living in the nonsense of the resurrection.

I tell you this morning — Jesus lives! And so can we. We can live radical new lives of faith and love. Jesus lives! And so can we. We can live changed lives filled with hope and joy. Jesus lives! And so can we!

He is risen! He is risen, indeed. Thanks be to God! Amen.

Being A
Good Doubter

He was a man, like any man, woman or child, who had many sides to him. There really are few, if any, one-dimensional people around. All of us are conglomerates of anger and love, of joy and sadness, of hope and despair, of faith and doubt. And as a member of the human race, he was just like that: a person of many qualities, capable of many feelings, thoughts and expressions.

One time, Jesus of Nazareth proposed to go to Bethany in Judea because his long-time friend, Lazarus, had died. A lot of his friends tried to persuade Jesus not to go. After all, it hadn't been that long ago that the people of that region had tried to stone him. It may not have been a safe place to go back to. But Jesus was resolute, and so our man-of-many-sides stood up and announced: "Let us also go, that we may die with him." Here was a loyal friend in the face of danger.

On another occasion, Jesus was teaching his followers about his impending death. This same loyal friend was confused and was seeking to understand the teaching. Of all those present, he was the one to interrupt and ask candidly: "Lord, we do not know where you are going; how can we know the way?" He wanted desperately to understand because he wanted to follow. The loyal friend was also the honest questioner and seeker.

He was also a man of commitment. Throughout the first 13 chapters of the book of Acts, we find his name among those who gathered in fellowship and prayer. He was among those gifted with the Holy Spirit and sent to preach. He was among those who, after Jesus' death and resurrection, devoted the rest of their lives to teaching and fellowship in Jesus' name. This loyal friend and honest questioner was also a devoted disciple.

Would it surprise you to know that the anonymous person I have been referring to is Thomas? Yes, Thomas: loyal friend, honest questioner, devoted disciple, doubter. And we all know that it's that last label that has stuck with his memory. Mention the name of Thomas and a simple word association occurs — ah yes, *doubting* Thomas.

But why? We have already noted that Thomas, like any of us, is more than one-dimensional; he is more than any one label can describe. Why, then, of all his good qualities, has he been painted with one word? Perhaps it is because Christians have been led to believe that doubt is not only wrong, but there is evil in it. Somewhere along the way we've been taught that a radical dichotomy exists between faith and doubt. Faith is good and doubt is bad. Faith builds up and doubt destroys. Faith nurtures and doubt stifles.

Perhaps it is time that we ask if there can be any meaningful faith, any gutsy faith, where no doubt has preceded it. Can we really know, for instance, the exhilaration that comes from suddenly becoming aware of God's presence in our lives without first knowing the torturous ache of God's absence? Can faith ever take on real depth and meaning without the honest wrestling that questions of doubt force upon us? The question is not whether doubt is good or bad. The question is whether faith can take root in anything else. The time is long past for us to quit avoiding our doubts by flogging Thomas' memory. My friends in Christ, Thomas is us, and perhaps his story tells us more about faith than it does about doubt.

Recall the story for a moment. Thomas was absent from the gathering of the disciples when Jesus first appeared to them following that first Easter sunrise. He had been a faithful follower during Jesus' ministry. We can only guess where he was and what he was doing. But it's a safe guess to say he was off somewhere grieving. He had been captured by this vision of a new kingdom Jesus talked about. He had seen the miracles of healing; he had witnessed changed hearts and lives; he had taken an active role in the shaping of the dream. And it had been killed on a cross. Despair? Yes! Grief? Certainly. Doubt? Probably. Perhaps he was out somewhere wandering the countryside trying to make sense of the tragedy at Golgotha which had jarred every fiber of his being. There were doubts, for sure, and they were honest doubts. What happened to the dream? Was it all a big masquerade? How can this kingdom of peace come from the darkness of this night?

Is it any wonder, then, that when he brought himself, in the midst of his questions and grief and doubt, to return to his friends, that he was totally unprepared for their excitement? "We have seen the Lord!" they shouted to him, and Thomas, in his moment of darkness, could only respond: "Unless I see in his hands the print of the nails, and place my finger in the mark of the nails, and place my hand in his side, I will not believe." Is it any wonder, my friends? Who wants to be set-up twice for disappointment and hurt? Who wants to get one's hopes up again only to have them destroyed by the reality of a cruel world? Doubts? You bet! Honest doubts born of believing with all one's heart in someone, in a dream, and seeing it cruelly shattered right before one's eyes.

But it was eight days later, and Thomas was about to climb out of his valley of despair and grief. Jesus came to his followers again with his greeting, "Peace be with you." And then, in that classic scene from scripture, Jesus turned to Thomas and gave him his chance to touch the wounds. Can you imagine the pathos of that moment? Thomas, in that moment of reborn hope and rekindled faith, responded with the highest confession we find in John's gospel: "My Lord and my God!" The highest confession in John's gospel sprang from the deepest despair.

Thomas is no culprit. He is not a rogue or a scoundrel. But rather he is us. Out of the reality of doubt, the possibility for faith is born. And here we need a word of caution. Even the faith that is forged by despair and born anew in the resurrection is not immune to doubt. We will always live with the paradox of faith and doubt as two sides of the same coin we call our lives. And the reason for this is quite obvious. Resurrection faith does not come to us like a package in the mail or a gift from grandma at Christmas. We can never possess it as such, for one possesses things and faith is not a thing; it is an experience. Like Thomas, when our experience of God begins to wane, we long for proof to beat away the gnawing doubts. We want hard evidence, something we can cling to. Yet, faith always comes as a challenge, as venture, as risk and as such, can't ever be totally captured for all times and all places in one moment. Even God and our feeble attempts to understand him, eludes us because every time we try to point to where he is, he moves on. Thus, the decision to believe is one that entails risk. We are those who "have not seen and yet have believed." We are those who live our lives in the midst of this doubt and faith, this death and resurrection dialectic and it is there that we learn what it means to walk with our God.

The issue for us is never, therefore, one of avoiding our doubts as if that will cure us of them. Thomas Carlyle once wrote: "The credibility gap in our communications with God is evident in the way we launder our thoughts and feelings so our prayers present no hint of doubt, no trace of question, and no scents of anger — and only half our hearts."

No, the issue for us is how to be good doubters; how to walk like Thomas honestly into the middle of them, no matter how scary and alone that feels, so that we can encounter the living God and have our own faith resurrected. It is a paradox, like losing one's life to find it, that doesn't make rational sense — until we live it. And then, out of the dust of honest doubt can be born the greatest expression of faith: "My Lord and my God."

A pastor I know told me recently that he saw one such miracle happen in the life of a 15-year-old girl during a weekend retreat. Quiet, reserved, shy, brilliant and troubled: that's how he described her. All weekend, he said, the hollow, lifeless eyes searched for answers to the gnawing questions that had eroded her life and spirit and made her appear dark and despondent. But something happened: Her eyes became more restless and alert. She was searching and she somehow knew she was close to something.

The group had spent the weekend on the theme "Discovery" and had talked about discovery of self, of others, and of God. And as another 15-year-old shared the pain of her older sister's recent suicide, the dam broke and water, like baptism, washed a face that hadn't cried in a very long time.

Later on that evening, the group did a Bible study around Luke 9 where Jesus asked his disciples: "Who do people say that I am?" And later in the chapter where Jesus lays out the conditions for discipleship: "If any want to become my followers, let them deny themselves and take up their cross daily and follow me. For those who want to save their life will lose it, and those who lose their life for my sake will save it." When the pastor asked the group what that sounded like — a commercial, a Sunday school lesson, a parent laying down another rule — the young girl with the tear-stained face responded: "It sounds to me like something worth giving my life to."

My pastor friend said to me in telling this story, "I sat with Thomas that night in the form of a 15-year-old girl and we shared some bread and wine in the presence of our Lord, Jesus Christ."

Do you see? Out of the struggle with honest doubt, a faith can be reborn, and new life can begin. Amen.

The Tiger
At The Edge

There is an ancient folktale about a tiger that is brought up with a herd of goats. From the day his eyes opened all he saw was a goat's life, so it became his style of life, too. The tiger munched grass with the rest, butted heads with the younger goats for recreation, and learned to bleat in an odd sort of way a sound that resembled, or so he thought, a goat's voice. Once in a while there was a nagging voice inside him that said, "You don't belong to this life!" But always, he put it aside as fantasy, some disturbing intrusion from the world of dreams. If his present life didn't satisfy him, he just marked it off as the discontent that always hovers around the edges of any lifestyle. So, he, a tiger, stayed with the goat's way of life because he believed that was the way life had to be.

Then one day a tiger came into the clearing. He was all tiger, having grown up knowing who he was. He looked into the clearing and spotted the goats. He roared the earth-shaking roar of his species, bounded out and made his kill. The goats fled in terror. But the tiger who had grown up with them stopped. He wanted to stay. The roar from the edge of the forest had stirred some lost memory deep inside of him. He flexed his automatic reflex to the challenge from the forest edge. The tiger at the edge had awakened in him a life he had never known but for which he had been created.

71

And so it was that the disciples after the resurrection went back to Galilee. The 21st chapter of John really forms a sort of epilogue to the resurrection story, but an important one. It's as if the writer has something very important to add to the story and, after what seems like the ending of the Gospel of John in the 20th chapter, appears to start a whole new story.

And what do those disciples do back in Galilee? Well, it appears that they aren't sure what it is they are supposed to be doing. Jesus sent them there, but now they seem lost, again, without his presence and guidance. So, they go fishing; they go back to the ordinary routines of their lives.

And what happens? Verse three tells us: "that night they caught nothing." Then, from the edge of the shore line, a voice calls to them to cast their nets on the other side of their boat. Scripture doesn't tell us why they listen to that voice. Maybe it had a familiar ring of authority to it. Maybe they were willing to try anything new to catch some fish. We just don't know, but we do know the result: a huge, huge catch of fish. And then they know the voice: "It is the Lord!"

You see, these disciples are like us in our endeavors to do things our way and on our own. They had gone from the joy of resurrection back to the ordinariness of their lives, and nothing had changed very much. They had been called to a new life from the edge of humanity by a voice that empowered them and gave them a new way of doing things. But they chose, instead, to be like the tiger who thought he was a goat. And it was the voice from the shore that called them, again, to the new life — a life in which fishing (that metaphor for evangelism) is successful because it listens to and is responsive to the one who calls us to the task.

In his book, *Remember Who You Are,* William H. Willimon of Duke University says that he recalls one thing his mother always told him whenever he left the house to go on a date during his high school days. As he left the house, she would stand at the front door and call after him, "Will, don't forget who you are."

We know what Mom Willimon meant, don't we? She didn't think Will was in danger of forgetting his name and street address. But she knew that, alone on a date, or in the midst of some party, or while joined by friends, he might forget who he was. She knew that sometimes all of us are tempted to answer to some alien name and to be who we are not. "Don't forget who you are," was the maternal benediction.

The disciples that morning as they fished without success were called from the shore by one who was calling them back to who they were. They were his children. They were his with a mission to do. And that mission would not and could not be successful without his guidance and presence.

These post-resurrection stories of Jesus which we focus on this week after Easter help remind us of who we are. They help validate the stories of the resurrection for the early Christian community, to be sure. But they serve to do much more than that. These stories help remind us.

Sure, Easter has come and gone. The resurrection was celebrated with the proper pomp and spirit. But now what?

Well, we listen to the voice from the shore urging us to be about his business. That's a good reminder for our community as well as for those first disciples.

Don't you see? These Easter stories give the Christian community stories to share. And those stories remind us of who is our focus and what is our mission. They tell us of Jesus' continual call to his people to serve him by pulling people into community in his name. And we do that by sharing the stories of resurrection which we know and have experienced.

Don't you see? We can never go back to the ordinary once we have heard that voice from the shore. We have been captured by a person who loves us and won't let us go. We have been captured by a story so powerful that we have been changed by its telling. And now, we must tell that story.

And we dare never make it boring! Robert McAfee Brown, professor of theology and ethics at the Pacific School of Religion, said it better than I can in his book, *Creative Dislocation — The Movement of Grace.* He writes:

73

Our faith does not come to us initially as theology, and particularly not as "systematic theology," but as story. Tell me about God: "Well, once upon a time there was a garden ..." Tell me about Jesus: "Well, once upon a time a little boy was born in a smelly stable in Bethlehem ..." Tell me about salvation: "Well, when this same boy grew up, he loved people so much that the rulers began to be frightened of him, and you know what they did? ..." Tell me about the church, "Well, there were a great many people who worked together: Mary and Priscilla and Martin Luther and Martin Luther King, Jr., and John and Sister Teresa, and you know what they did? ..."[1]

Don't forget who you are! We are the ones named and claimed in the baptismal waters. We are Christ's people. People of the resurrection. People who fish for a living among one another. People who have a story to share and a faith to proclaim. That's who we are.

The voice from the water's edge called them out of the ordinariness of their lives, to a new life and a new mission. The church of today needs to hear and heed that same voice.

And notice what Jesus did when they got to shore? He fed them. It was a meal of thanksgiving in fellowship with Christ. It is a meal we enjoy when we gather around bread and wine. It is a meal for nourishment and hope. It is a meal that fills us with love and forgiveness and strength — for going from here to tell the most important story any person ever needs to hear.

Can you hear that call to a new life? Amen.

---

1. Robert McAfee Brown, *Creative Dislocation — The Movement of Grace,* (Nashville, Abingdon Press, 1980), pp. 130-131.

Life Insurance Available
— Free, But Not Cheap

It is reported that during World War II, a young bomber pilot, just before taking off on a critical mission, lit a match in the presence of the chaplain, and, after having blown it out, asked him, "Now, tell me, man to man, is that all that happens to us when we die?" Peggy Lee, several years ago, asked something of the same question in her plaintive song: "Is this all there is?"

The question is as old as Job and those before him, "If a person die, can they live again?" And we are back again to the questions of what life is all about, what happens after death, and, indeed, what is the meaning of our existence — questions for which answers come hard, assurances are often shallow and, all too often, we are left with that question still burning in our mouths as we bury a father, or mother, or husband, or friend — "Is this all there is?"

We are a strange people, indeed. Living as we do in a land of affluence, where most of us want for very little, we feel compelled to develop programs that will secure our futures. With the usual American ingenuity, we have designed insurance programs that can cover almost every calamity we can name, and even some we can't. We fear our futures: What will become of me, where will I live, what is life all about anyway? But we also fear today, so we build fancy and elaborate security systems around ourselves and around our possessions.

It can be a tragic and sad life if all we see is here and now, and all our efforts must go into protecting the "stuff" we accumulate around us. Unfortunately, many people fail to grasp that life insurance policies can never really answer the basic existential questions that most of us wrestle with at sometime during our lives.

But there is good news for us. Believe it or not, there is a life insurance plan available for you and me that is more comprehensive than any plan you could ever buy from an agent; there is a plan available for us that is written out so simply and clearly, that a child can grasp it, often before the parents ever can; and the best news of all — it's free! It is a plan that, as you stand before open graves in airy cemeteries under green canopies, we read from. Listen: "Blessed are the dead who die in the Lord . . . I am the Resurrection and the life. Those who believe in me, even though they die, will live, and everyone who lives and believes in me will never die." A life insurance plan that guarantees that life does not end. A life insurance plan that offers more security than you and I can ever imagine; more peace of mind now and for those left standing beside graves years after dirt is piled on caskets.

Here is the good news for us. Our God loves us so much that he sent his son, Jesus the Christ, who died on a cross for us and rose to new life three days later so that we might have new life now and in the future. The life insurance plan is free for us: the premium was already paid by Jesus with his own life! It is not a cheap plan. It cost our Lord; but it is complete and comprehensive and free, and offered to all of us.

So, Peggy Lee, sing your song and ask your question: "Is this all there is?" As for me, I'll live my life under God's life insurance plan, not because it's free, but because God gave it to me — signed, sealed, and delivered by Jesus the Christ.

Now, I have trouble understanding why more folks don't "buy into" this plan for their lives. And I'm not talking necessarily about people outside of the walls and fellowship of our churches. If they haven't accepted this good news maybe it's more our fault than theirs. Maybe we haven't told the story clearly and plainly enough, or often enough. Maybe we haven't lived the story we tell. They see us talk of love and fellowship and caring for one another, and then they see us fight over whether we should serve wine or grape juice for communion, or fighting over who's in and who's out of the kingdom as if that is our decision, or they see us fighting over whether we like the pastor or not. Maybe we haven't lived the story we tell — we talk of love, and live in unlove; we talk of trust and live in quiet solitude; we talk of unity and live in division. But I can understand this. We are all sinners and our fellowship will reflect that from time to time. We must work at this forgiveness and grace stuff.

No, my problem is not with those out there for whom the gospel, the good news, is unclear. My problem is with those who have heard and yet fail to grasp the message for them. To put it into the framework of this sermon — those who want to write their own life insurance plans because they can't or won't accept the one God offers them in Christ. Somehow, the good news can't be received as good news. To put it even more plainly: I have trouble understanding why anyone would want to work out their own salvation, to work and sweat and struggle and fret to get into the kingdom of God. We are saved by what he did, not by what we try to do! It's God's grace, his unconditional love for us, that is our life insurance plan, and all we have to do to have it is accept it as the gift it is.

Well. Maybe that is our problem: We don't know how to accept gifts. Somewhere along the line we are taught that it's not polite to accept gifts without putting up some kind of fuss, "Oh, no, I couldn't accept that. You shouldn't have." And all the time, in the back of our minds we're thinking, "Why is she doing this? Why am I getting this gift? What does he want from me? I'd better be careful, there's got to be a string attached here somewhere. If I take this, then I'm going to have to give something back in return and I really don't have time today to go shopping." And on and on, our untrusting, selfish little minds go.

Why can't we be like children? Ever see a child accept a gift? No hedging there — eyes light up as if a thousand lights had been turned on in the head; smiles stretch farther than the limitations of face and ears would seem to allow; eager hands reach out and acceptance is immediate and real and wonderful. No complications. No internal wrestling. No guilt.

Maybe we can take a lesson there as we hear the good news offered to us.

You know, after reading the gospel lesson from John 10 over and over again this week, I discovered that people back in Jesus' time had trouble too with accepting who Jesus was. Here Jesus was walking around on Solomon's porch in the temple at Jerusalem on the day of the Feast of Dedication. At this festive occasion, called the Festival of Lights, Jesus was standing in this portico of the east side of the temple. And, inquirers sought him out and asked him about whether he was the Messiah or not. It was not a question asked in honest sincerity or truth. He had been showing them all along and they still came and wanted more proof before they could accept it.

And Jesus answered them: "I have told you, and you do not believe. The works that I do in my Father's name testify to me." And there lies the tragedy which is unbelief: "I have told you, and you do not believe."

Jesus had announced the good news in word and deed, in miracle and teaching, on hillside and in temple, and still, people could not believe. In contrast to those who wanted to make God's love something we must earn by adherence to law after law, ritual after ritual, Jesus claimed that God loved even the sinner. It was the righteous, the religious of Jesus' day who had trouble hearing that as good news. They had developed a whole system designed around earning God's love. They somehow could not grasp the truth that God was greater than their systems, and more loving than they could ever imagine. So they rejected Jesus and his teachings.

78

So what say you? We have heard the good news time and time again from this pulpit and church. What say you?

Maybe we need to hear the children sing again, "Jesus loves me," for there is the message as simple as the gift is for us. Amen.

Getting
By Giving

Solomon Grundy,
Born on Monday,
Christened on Tuesday,
Married on Wednesday,
Took ill on Thursday,
Worse on Friday,
Died on Saturday,
Buried on Sunday.
This is the end of Solomon Grundy.

It is an old nursery rhyme that some of you may recall. Now, I'm not suggesting that we use it to replace the gospel text for today, but I did begin with it because it picks up one of the central themes of our text: the shortness of life on this earth. Jesus said to his disciples: "I am with you only a little longer." In fact, throughout this section of John's gospel, from chapter 13 through 17, this section we call the Final Discourse of Jesus, this theme of the shortness of life is reiterated again and again. Jesus seems to be emphasizing to his disciples, since they were the objects of this discourse, that life is short and that he would only be with them for a short time.

If we looked at the beginning of this 13th chapter of John, we would see immediately that Jesus is right. Judas had just left the last supper to betray him, and he knew that in a short time he would be separated from his friends, arrested, tried and crucified. For Jesus, at this point, death was his destiny and not one that was very far off.

And looking at Jesus' life and ministry, it was, indeed, a short time. His ministry covered but a short span of three years or less, depending on which gospel account you follow. The life he lived was but 33 years as best we can determine: a short life by any standards.

So, one of the points Jesus seems to be making throughout this discourse is that we should make the most of the time that we have. He seems to be saying to his disciples: "Pay attention! We haven't got long and you need to hear what I have to say."

Anyone who has had a serious illness or has lost someone close to them knows only too well how short life can be. I hear again and again, the sadness that people face in the death of loved ones over those things that were left unsaid or undone because we just didn't get around to them. We always thought there would be time later. Or, we were too stubborn to put our egos aside and risk resolutions where avoidance had been the order of the day.

So, the question becomes, how do we make the most of the life that we have? With life being all too brief, how do we get the most out of life?

The world has an answer. The world tells us to "go for it"; to "live life to the fullest"; to "reach for the golden ring"; to "grab for what we can get." We've heard those answers. We hear them constantly in the commercials on television. We are told that life can be full and we can get the most out of it if we "go for it." Just listen to the message behind the advertising push to buy or use a particular product, and that is precisely what you will hear. Life is short, so live it to the max.

Now, the gospel has a different answer. How do we get the most out of life? By losing it. By giving it away. Jesus said no less than 13 times: "The person who seeks to save his (or her) life will lose it, but whoever loses his life, that is whoever gives it away, doesn't try to hoard it, doesn't seek to hold it it tightly, whoever loses his life will find it." And to make the point even clearer, this Jesus showed everybody who had eyes to see and ears to hear just what it meant. He gave himself away for others again and again and again. He was, as some have dubbed him, a "man for others." His first miracle at Cana was to make people happy at a wedding feast. His last miracle was to replace Malchus' ear so that he would be whole again. And he never counted the cost of giving himself to and for others — even to giving his life on that cross.

Do we want to get the most out of life? Then we need to hear the message of the gospel that encourages us to give it away — because only by doing that can we really find out what life is all about. It is the paradox of Christian living, and it is true.

In sermon preparation this week, I ran across a wonderful fable titled "The Dance of the Heart." It is a fitting parable for the message of the gospel to us this morning.

Once upon an ancient time in a distant land lived an emperor and an empress, who had a son and a daughter. The children, as children will, often quarrelled and nagged each other in ways that distressed their wise and loving parents. They often argued about who would get the larger inheritance.

"Perhaps we have spoiled them," said their mother. "They are too often concerned only for themselves."

"This is not a good quality for future generations," said their father. And so the parents discussed how to prepare their children to be the next rulers of the kingdom.

When the children were old enough, the emperor and the empress called them to the throne room. "Our gift to you is a wheat field ready for sowing," they said. "The harvest of your hearts at the end of the growing season will tell us if you are ready to take your rightful place in the kingdom."

The children weren't sure if they understood their parents' wishes, but they did understand farming, and set off, delighted, to plant and tend the field. They worked very hard together, which wasn't always easy. When their first harvest came in, they were proud indeed.

"See the wheat we have grown with our own hands! Let us build a storage place for the grain. Then we will have some for now and some for later. Perhaps this is the lesson we are to learn." So they set about to build a barn in which to store their harvest.

The day came for the emperor and empress to visit. "Mother and Father," said the young prince, "see the wheat we have grown and how much we have saved for the winter!"

"Very good, my children," said the emperor. "Your minds are certainly working. Your hearts, however, are still sleeping. We will come to visit you again next year."

Once again the children plowed and planted. Once again they had a good harvest. When they gathered their grain, they said, "Let us put some away and trade the rest for other goods." They hurried to the marketplace, where they bartered their grain for many things, and then took their treasures home. "Now," they said, "let us give our parents gifts for all their kindness."

The parents came for their annual visit and once again inspected the work of their children. They received their gifts and thanked the prince and princess warmly. "My children," said the mother, "your hearts are no longer sleeping. Your hearts have learned to walk; now, you must let them dance. We will come again next year."

When harvest time came the children were puzzled. What were they to do with this year's harvest? They decided once again to save some of the crop and to take the rest to the market place. "This time let us not be in such a hurry," the young prince suggested. And so they set out.

On the road they met a mother and two bouncing children carrying their grain to market. Just as the prince and princess were about to pass them, the children tripped their mother and all three tumbled to the ground. The grain in the woman's basket tipped over, and the wind blew most of it away. The children grew silent, and the mother did not get up.

"Here," said the young princess rushing to her aid, "let me help you."

But the woman said, "It is no use. All that I have has danced away in the wind. Now my children will be hungry when winter comes."

The small children tried to comfort their mother. "It's all right," they said. "The wind has given the grain to the birds. They are hungry, too."

The dance of the wind brought back the words of the emperor and empress. Suddenly, the prince and princess saw with new eyes. "We shall share our grain with you," they said at once. They hurried to pour some of their grain into the woman's basket, and helped her on her way.

After the family had gone, the young prince said to his sister, "My heart has skipped a beat! I do not know," he continued, "if that is from its dancing, or from fear that we will not have enough grain for ourselves when we get to the marketplace."

"When two people dance," the princess wisely replied, "one person leads and the other follows. If we let love lead and fear follows, then our hearts can dance without tripping. Let us practice this step in the marketplace."

And so they did. To their surprise, they saw many people in the marketplace in need of one thing or another. They gave a little grain here or a bartered good there or an act of kindness somewhere else. Each time they gave, they found their hearts no longer skipped quite so anxiously. At the end of the day, their baskets were considerably lighter — but so were their hearts.

When the emperor and empress saw how the young prince and princess had begun to share their gifts with all who lived in the kingdom, they finally trusted them to rule. The children never forgot the lesson they learned. Each year, their love led them to give a little more, and to keep a little less. And their hearts danced.

I realize that the sermon this morning sounds dangerously close to being a stewardship sermon (and here you thought it was safe to come to church in spring). If that's how it sounded to you, then, perhaps, you have heard it correctly because the Christian life is the life of stewardship. Someone once said that stewardship is everything we do after we say, "We believe!" And the paradox of Christian living is very simply that we get the most out of life when we learn to give it away and not clutch it to ourselves in feverish concern for self.

We get by giving. And, as the story goes, our hearts will learn to dance. Amen.

The Peace
That Invades

It was not like they had anticipated.
  It was supposed to be a celebration —
    a celebration of deliverance as they remembered the
      Passover in that upper room.
But Jesus had upset them — with his actions and with his
  words.
  Before the meal even began,
    he knelt before each one of them with towel and water
      insisting on washing the grime from their feet —
      it was the action of a common servant,
        and yet, most intimate.
  Then, after the meal, he made predictions that shocked
    them:
    "I'm telling you the truth, one of you is going to betray
      me."
    "My friends, I shall not be with you very much longer."
    And to Peter, the rock, he said: "Before the rooster crows
      you will say three times that you do not know me."
Those disciples sat in stunned silence.
  What Jesus had just said to them
    shook them to the timbers of their faith.
And so, they probably never heard his words of promise;
  they were probably too confused to comprehend the gift

he gave them when he said:
"Peace I leave with you; my peace I give to you. . .
Do not let your hearts be troubled, and do not let them
be afraid."
And I will dare to say that we can identify with those disciples.
How many of us, upon receiving shocking news, hear well-
meaning
neighbors and friends mouth the platitudes:
"Everything'll be all right."
"She's better off."
"Everything will work out for the best."
And how many of us, in the midst of a life tragedy,
really believe any of that?
Do you know the experience?
Circumstances cause our worlds to fall apart — death,
accident, announcement that the disease is terminal,
divorce.
And life falls apart at the seams,
and somebody standing on the sidelines,
wanting to be helpful, mouths the pious pronouncement:
"It'll all work out; God will give you comfort and
peace."
Like the disciples, we aren't ready to accept,
to hear,
to comprehend what those words mean.
And yet, there isn't one among us who doesn't *need*
what Jesus offered his first disciples.
When life is in a state of confusion:
personal relationships are at the straining point,
job pressures seem more than we can bear,
family and friends offer little support
to the lonely, hurting person inside.
And "peace" is what we need — some respite from the
frustrations, some solace from the pressures,
some relief from the inner turmoils.

But where does peace come from?
Certainly not from the world.

The prescription written in the world for peace is synthetic:
  alcohol, pills, increased leisure —
  all human-made, all contrived, all illusory to real peace
    as we need it.
As someone has profoundly quipped: "There is no problem
  so bad that drinking and drugs can't make worse."
We can read the testimonies about people
  who fought their way out of chemical jungles,
    or who battled the bottle and defeated it,
    or who accumulated "things" as a way to gain inner
      peace
  and their confessions stand crystal clear:
    "We can't make, drink, buy or swallow peace."
True peace,
  of heart, of mind, of spirit,
    is a gift.
It is a gift that bursts through the walls we erected,
  a gift that shoves open the stuffy windows of our dark
    nights,
    a gift that invades our lives.
Saint Augustine said it long ago:
  "You have made us for yourself.
  Our souls are restless until they find their rest in Thee,
    O Lord."
True peace comes
  only as Jesus Christ invades our lives
    as the Prince of Peace,
    and we cannot manufacture or buy it — it is a gift.
Jesus said it to his confused, scared, shocked disciples:
  "My peace I give to you."
And Jesus says it to us today —
  confused by the events of cruelty we see inflicted upon
  the helpless of the world;
    scared by the economic times and the uncertainties
    it has brought;
      shocked by personal tragedies happening in lives
      all around us daily.

Jesus says to you and me:
"My peace I give to you. I do not give
to you as the world gives."

There would be little hope for us today
if there wasn't a grave distinction
between the peace the world gives,
and that which comes from the "Prince of Peace."
How often the ears of the world have heard the vain promises:
"This is the war to end all wars."
How could we have dreamed the dreams of peace by building
world organizations such as the "United Nations" and
calling together "Peace Keeping Forces."
How often we have listened to the rhetoric of world leaders
claim that peace can be insured through greater arms,
more powerful bombs, larger defense budgets.
We have listened, we have acquiesced, we have nodded
hopefully —
but peace still eludes us.

Jesus has said that his peace is quite different.
It is a gift;
it comes not with promises of a better life
but in the midst of present life to make it better.
There is a story of a young family living in Europe during
World War II.
Those were frightening days to live, to be sure.
Bombs rained daily on homes and lives.
This family of four, I had read about,
had made very detailed plans of what they would do
in case of an alert.
The father would take the small son;
the mother would take care of the infant daughter,
and they would head for the nearest bomb shelter.
One night, during the great confusion of such an alert,
the family became separated.
When the all clear was given, the father and son searched
frantically for the mother and daughter.

They returned to their home to see the roof gutted by a bomb
   and there, under the rubble, were the dead bodies of the
      mother and daughter.
   For some strange reason, they never got to the shelter.
The husband collapsed in grief.
   But as he wept,
      he suddenly discovered his son was missing.
   Desperately he looked for his boy and found him out in the
      garden looking quietly up at the sky.
   Silently, the father stood beside his son
      and took his hand into his own.
   Looking up at his father,
      the little boy said,
         "It's going to be all right, Father. God is hanging
            out the stars again."
The father claimed that faith was born in him at that moment
   and his spirit was flooded with peace.
      He recalled the words of Jesus,
         "When things are at their worst, look up,
            for your salvation is at hand."[1]

That kind of peace the world can neither give nor promise.
   It is a peace that can come
      only from the One who gave his life
         so that we can have life.
   It is peace that
      allows us to live and love
         in a world of international tension and conflict;
         that enables us to look at the needs of our neighbors
            even when it's painful to see distended bellies
            on small children,
         or the loneliness in the widow's eyes.
   It is a peace that invades the closed circles of our private
      worlds
      and says, "Do not be afraid."
   It is, friends in Christ,
      the peace of God, given in Jesus the Christ,
         that passes all our attempts at understanding.

91

It is a gift —
    for troubled hearts,
        for confused minds,
            for anxious spirits.
Hear and receive these gentle words of Jesus:
    "Peace I give to you."

                                                    Amen

---

1. Paul M. Werger, "Peace At Last," *Augsburg Sermons: Gospels, Series C,* (Minneapolis, Augsburg Publishing House, 1973), p. 148.

A Promise
Is Given

It took me a long time to figure out what it was about that gospel text just read that bothered me. I read and re-read the last two chapters in Luke until it finally hit me.

I want to lead you to that same revelation, so let's do a review of the events in Jesus' life, or should I say death.

Jesus was crucified, dead, and buried. Let us begin there. And there can be no mistake about that fact. The Roman garrison whose business it was to do such things was very efficient. They knew when a person was dead.

Those who had been followers of this Jesus for three years also knew he was dead. They had been around, watching in anguish as their gentle leader said but few words from his lonely pedestal-cross. They watched as the sagging body was finally taken down and their friend carried away to a borrowed tomb. But their pain was more than the suffering of grief one feels when someone close dies. Their pain went into the fibre of their souls, into the very center of their beings as Jews, for this was to be the Messiah, the Christ. This Jesus was to be the one sent from God to free them once and for all from their oppressors. So, their tears and anguish were for dreams torn apart as well as for a man spread apart on a cross. That cross had killed hope and where hope dies, there is really no life at all. That cross took away from them a man they not only loved, but one they bet their futures on.

But the story didn't end there, thank God. For those who know the story of the resurrection and have heard it retold these past few weeks, know that some of the women who had followed Jesus went to the tomb to pay their last respects and to do the customary anointing of the body. What they found both startled and puzzled them. The tomb was empty and they heard the good news that Jesus was, indeed, not dead, but risen. They remembered then his promise that on the third day he would rise. They must have gotten hysterical with joy and ran to tell the others. There they stood, all out of breath, talking all at once about an empty tomb and two strange men who reminded them of Jesus' words and all giddy and giggly again as hope rushed in to find a home in their sorrowful hearts. And the disciples had trouble believing this wild story. In fact, they didn't believe it, dismissing it as an idle tale told by hysterical females in the midst of grief that was obviously too much for them to handle.

Well, fortunately, the story doesn't end there either, for if it did we'd have the rational guys against those always irrational girls argument all over again with Easter being a rehearsal of the old, time-worn feud between the genders. Maybe God knew that would happen, so Jesus made a few more appearances, this time to the more rational side of the house — the men.

First, there is that marvelous story where Jesus appeared to two of his followers on the Emmaus road and they didn't recognize him. There they were all depressed and sad telling the story of Jesus, to Jesus, and they didn't even know it was him until . . . until he broke bread and gave it to them, and in that all too familiar act, they recognized him.

Then the Gospel of Luke, from which the accounts we are recalling today come, the Gospel of Luke records the final appearance and this is where we stand this night.

As these two who had seen Jesus on the Emmaus road were telling their story back in Jerusalem, Jesus suddenly and unexpectedly appeared in their midst. Luke tells us they were "startled and frightened." They thought they were seeing a ghost. After all, Jesus was dead. Jesus showed them his hands and his feet and said, "Touch me, handle me, see for yourselves."

I like what scripture says then: "And while they still disbelieved for joy, and wondered." Isn't that a great phrase: "while they disbelieved for joy." That's like when we get all excited about seeing an old friend we haven't seen for years and we get all beside ourselves and we say in our excitement: "I can't believe it! I can't believe it's really you!" That's disbelieving for joy.

Well, while the disciples stood around with their jaws open muttering, "I can't believe it! It's him! I can't believe it!" Jesus sat and ate and that clinched it. They had seen him eat with them many times and this was Jesus. And as they gathered around him, Jesus began teaching again. He used this last appearance to interpret his resurrection as the fulfillment of the scriptures. And then — he ascended or, as scripture reads, "was carried up into heaven."

Now, here comes my puzzlement. It is recorded that the disciples "worshipped him, and returned to Jerusalem with great joy."

Doesn't that strike you as rather odd? It did me. These were the folks who were devastated by the events of Good Friday. And here they were about to lose their great and faithful friend again — this time forever. Why would they be happy about that?

We all know that even small goodbyes can be heart-wrenching. How many of us have stood at airports or at train terminals and kissed loved ones goodbye with tears and waves and fears?

But the Festival of the Ascension is upbeat, with the focus more on Jesus' enthronement at the Father's right hand rather than on the disciples' separation anxiety. A sense of parting, of losing what they had just so joyfully found, seems inevitable. Yet, the evangelist does not mention tearful farewells, last-minute pleas for Jesus to "stay just a little bit longer," or the numbing of grief setting in afterward. Luke writes, "They returned to Jerusalem with great joy, and spent all their time in the temple praising God." Mark, who also records this event, reports, "They went out to make their proclamation everywhere, and the Lord worked with them and confirmed their words by the miracles that followed."

Why was this parting so different? That was the mystery I couldn't resolve. Then I read again the words that I had somehow overlooked in other readings. Just before the ascension, Jesus turns to his beloved followers and says: "I am sending upon you what my Father promised; so stay here in the city until you have been clothed with power from on high." You see? Jesus left them with a promise they could hold onto. True, he had promised and predicted before his death that he would rise again, and they didn't "hear" him. Certainly, the arrest and what followed was so awful, and the prospect of resurrection so preposterous, so bold and unthinkable, that they either rejected it or never really understood it all in the first place.

But this time . . . this time they heard the promise given, and it filled then with hope and joy and excitement.

Maybe we can understand this in our own human way as well. Ever have someone go away for a time, but they leave something with you to remember them? It is like the object which is left — a picture, a shirt that carries the scent of the person's favorite perfume or cologne, a favorite object of that person — it's like that object makes the person present, there, even when they are absent and far off somewhere. And that object not only reminds us of the person, but also serves as a comforting reminder of her or his return. It bridges the absence.

Well, the promise given to those first believers did the same thing. Jesus comforted the disciples with his promise of the Spirit, who would "clothe them with power from above." And when that Spirit came, they could be about the work of the kingdom, which is, of course, what all of us should be about until he comes again.

As followers of this King today, we continue to get power and comfort from the promise he made. Through the Spirit's action in word and sacrament, Jesus is with us. While we still long for his return and the fullness of the kingdom we so need, we know that we can experience glimpses of it as we hold onto the gift, or shall we say, as the gift holds on to us in the meantime. Ascension is a celebration of the promise of the Spirit. And it is that promised gift which empowers, sustains, and gladdens us in this busy time of kingdom preparation between this ascension and his return in glory.

Now we know why those disciples were full of joy. Now we know why our hearts can sing on this night — for we have been given that same promise. And we know the gift it brings. Amen.

A Strange,
New Math

We have a wonderful mystery to contemplate this morning, and it is summarized in a strange formula. It's not really all that complicated, but it is worthy of reflection for it has implications for our lives together. Here is the formula, an equation, really: 1 + 1 + 1 = One.

Rather strange math, isn't it? Well, it's God's math, so let's see how it works.

That strange formula really comes from the gospel text for today. For the past several weeks during this Easter season, our gospel readings have come from that section of John's gospel known as the Final Discourse of Jesus. This last speech, if you will, that Jesus makes to his disciples concludes with these verses from the 17th chapter. It is really a prayer of Jesus to his Father in heaven and has often been called the High Priestly Prayer of Jesus. In a sense, it is Jesus' last will and testament, his parting shot, his last effort to teach, to exhort, to encourage, to empower his disciples.

Now for the math part. Listen to Jesus' words: "I ask not only on behalf of these, but also on behalf of those who will believe in me through their word, that they may all be one. As you, Father, are in me and I am in you, may they also be in us, so that the world may believe that you have sent me." Did you hear it? 1 + 1 + 1 = One. It's not too difficult, once we understand the parts of the equation. Let's unravel the mystery slowly.

Start with the first two parts of the equation: $1 + 1$. Remember Jesus' words: "You, Father, are in me and I am in you" and later he comments as he prays to his father, "We are one." $1 + 1$ — the Father and the Son are united. They are united in every way. They are united in will, in power, in loving intent for humankind, in commitment to salvation, in a mercy that endures forever. That's what Jesus is stating in his prayer. Jesus came that we might know God — his will, his intent, his love, his grace, his forgiveness, his power, his peace. Do you want to know what God is like? Look at Jesus. This is truly a case of "like father, like son" carried to the ultimate. To see and know one is to see and know the other. In God's strange, new math, $1 + 1$ is truly one.

Like the vertical dimension of the cross, God has reached down to this earth in his Son. He poured himself out in this man. $1 + 1$ became One, because "God so loved the world ..." (you know the rest of that scripture by heart).

But there is more to this mystery. There is another integer to consider. Jesus also said: I pray "that they may be one, as we are one, I in them and you in me, that they may become completely one." Who is "they"? You and me.

Using the image of the cross again, picture that horizontal beam. Imagine it growing and growing and extending its arms. Watch how those arms grow and stretch and bend until they curve in upon themselves and form this huge circle that includes you, and you, and you, and me, and our friends across the street, and over across the country, and over in Delaware, and Virginia, and England, and South Africa and Asia and ... just let those arms go and join hands.

There is really no magic to God's math — we are one in God! It sounds complicated only because our self-centeredness is offended by being lost in the oneness of others. We have been inundated with the 20th century philosophy of "I-ness," so that the concept of $1 + 1 + 1$ equaling One is somehow foreign to our sense of personhood. We somehow feel that it violates our individuality. But it's God's math, not reasoned calculus. It's God's math, not pop psychology. It's God's math, and it works.

And it works because of the heretofore unmentioned third divine partner linked to the first two — namely, the Holy Spirit. The Spirit accomplishes what God has ordained. The Spirit completes the work of God in Christ by calling us together, enlightening us with his Word, filling us with power through the sacraments, sending us out to gather others in his name and around the table with us. By his power, we are one — not by our own initiatives, not by our own creativities, not by our own inventions. We are God's, claimed in the waters of baptism, joined together in his body, the Church, and empowered for living as a community of faith — through his Spirit.

And this has some broad and far-reaching implications for us as a people and as a church. Let me just mention four briefly.

First, the fact that God's strange math works, that 1 + 1 + 1 = One, means that we are stronger together than we are apart. Think about that for a moment. We are stronger together than we are apart. Our ones equal one — a whole. The gifts that God has given each of us individually are to be joined together to benefit the whole. We are to be a living organism, a body, that works together in ways we cannot work apart. This means we need to share our gifts with one another. In fact, in the New Testament, whenever gifts are mentioned, they are always mentioned in the light and the context of the community. Only as God's gifts build up this community of faith are they being used as they were intended to be used. Read Paul in Corinthians or read Colossians. That's where it says it.

The second implication for God's strange math comes from the text itself. Why are we all to be one? Jesus answers: "So that the world may know that you have sent me and have loved them even as you have loved me." God's purpose is fulfilled in that math, you see. Our oneness is a witness to the world of who Jesus is. People look to us to understand Jesus. Why?

101

Because we claim to be his body. And further, the only way the world will know about his love for them is through us. We are the arms of the cross outstretched and growing, every time we join hands with others in love. Joined to Christ in baptism, we are joined with one another in his body, and we have the responsibility to reach out to others in that love and forgiveness and grace we have come to know and experience in this place.

Maybe we need to ask how well we do that? Or perhaps, how often? When was the last time we invited someone to worship with us? I'm fond of saying that it is the best invitation we can ever offer someone and I truly believe it — for where else in this world do you hear about a love so great that it keeps on accepting us each and every time we come, no matter where we have been or what we have done? Where else in this world do we find acceptance and peace that is not earned? Where else in this world do we hear good news that can literally change peoples' lives? So why, then, are we so reluctant to make that simple invitation? Be an inviter — it may change someone's life. The story of the Christian faith is filled with such lives. Yours and mine included.

The third implication of the truth of God's math has to do with our stance in the world. To believe, to really believe, that we are joined to Christ and to one another and can find wholeness and oneness in that union, puts us in direct opposition to the preaching of the world around us. I found a poignant example of that in a mail advertisement that came across my desk recently. It was titled "The Black Book of Executive Politics" and was written anonymously by "Z." This is actually what the advertisement said about this book.

> *Written by a world-class corporate infighter who prefers to remain anonymous, this priceless volume contains 87 street-smart hints, tips, short-cuts, ploys, strategies and approaches for surviving — and making it big in the company political arena ... People call company politics a "game." But it's a game you have to play, like it or not, if you want to survive and succeed.*

Listen to the contents of this book that is going to put me at the top of the corporate ladder:

> *Why style — rather than performance — is the key factor in determining who makes the boardroom.*
> *When teamwork isn't the answer.*
> *How to make points with the boss without being obviously on-the-make.*
> *How to learn needed inside information without being unethical.*

And it goes on and on. The letter inside the ad states: "I'm talking about truly Machiavellian stuff here. I know it all sounds a bit paranoid. But there are times when a little paranoia can give you the backside protection you need. You'll get the latest and most diabolical thinking on these political skills." And then he ends with two seemingly contradictory thoughts. First, he plants the seed about the opposition: "How many people in your company are sending away for their copies of the Black Book?" And then he said, that if I act right away, I'll get a free copy of "Creating a Loyal Staff." A loyal staff? After I've learned you want me to beat them up in the corporate arena and I'm not sure who is reading the same Black Book I am? Give me a break.

But there it is. What do you think "Z" would say about God's math?

Well, finally, a closing word about what this text doesn't mean. I've heard a lot of well-meaning people use this text on oneness as a pitch for a global church of some sort. There's no question that Christ's prayer calls for oneness, but it's hard to imagine that Jesus, in his last moments, was making a pitch for one international church or one world-wide mission board, or one universal hymnal. Those may be important human dreams, but Jesus was more concerned in the unity of spirit that would be about the Father's business. And what is that business? To a world of sinful people, we have a word of forgiveness. To a world that can't distinguish between right and wrong, we have truth in our proclamations. To a world that practices war, we announce a peace that goes beyond human understanding or engineering. What is the Father's business? It's about love and grace and justice that are more than words and slogans.

A closing story about what happens when the math doesn't work — when we don't allow it to work. It is reported that Mahatma Gandhi, in his younger days, was impressed with Christianity. One Sunday in South Africa he went to a church, planning to ask the minister afterwards for instructions in the faith. But as he entered the building the ushers refused to seat him. "Why don't you visit the colored peoples' church?" he was asked. Gandhi never became a Christian. "If Christians also have differences, I might as well remain a Hindu," he explained.

Yes, we have differences — but in God's strange math 1 + 1 + 1 = One. For those who believe that, their eyes look upon their neighbor in a whole new way. For those who believe that, their arms cannot help but reach out to join those who know the same math. For those who believe, God touches and blesses and makes them (us) one with him and with one another. Amen.

Books In This Cycle C Series

Gospel Set

When It Is Dark Enough
Sermons For Advent, Christmas And Epiphany
Charles H. Bayer

Walking To ... Walking With ... Walking Through
Sermons For Lent And Easter
Glenn E. Ludwig

The Divine Advocacy
Sermons For Pentecost (First Third)
Maurice A. Fetty

Troubled Journey
Sermons For Pentecost (Middle Third)
John Lynch

Extraordinary Faith For Ordinary Time
Sermons For Pentecost (Last Third)
Larry Kalajainen

First Lesson Set

The Days Are Surely Coming
Sermons For Advent, Christmas And Epiphany
Robert A. Hausman

Turning Obstacles Into Opportunities
Sermons For Lent And Easter
Rodney Thomas Smothers

Grapes Of Wrath Or Grace?
Sermons For Pentecost (First Third)
Barbara Brokhoff

Summer Fruit
Sermons For Pentecost (Middle Third)
Richard L. Sheffield

Stepping Inside The Story
Sermons For Pentecost (Last Third)
Thomas G. Rogers

DATE DUE

GAYLORD			PRINTED IN U.S.A.